Mikhail Chekhov as
Actor, Director, and Teacher

Theater and Dramatic Studies, No. 43

Oscar G. Brockett, Series Editor

Leslie Waggener Professor of Fine Arts
and Professor of Drama
The University of Texas at Austin

Other Titles in This Series

Mikhail Chekhov as
Actor, Director, and Teacher

by
Lendley C. Black

UMI Research Press

Ann Arbor, Michigan

Produced and distributed by
UMI Research Press
an imprint of
University Microfilms, Inc.
Ann Arbor, Michigan 48106

Library of Congress Cataloging in Publication Data

Black, Lendley C.
  Mikhail Chekhov as actor, director, and teacher.

  (Theater and dramatic studies ; no. 43)
  Revision of the author's thesis (Ph.D.)—
University of Kansas, 1984.
  Bibliography: p.
  Includes index.
  1. Chekhov, Michael, 1891-1955. 2. Actors—
Soviet Union—Biography. 3. Theatrical producers
and directors—Soviet Union—Biography. 4. Acting.
I. Title. II. Series.
PN2728.C45B55 1987   792'.028'0924 [B]   87-5995
ISBN 0-8357-1800-X (alk. paper)

For Connie

Contents

Preface

Mikhail Alexandrovich Chekhov was an important member of the group of great Russian theatre artists that flourished between 1898 and the late 1920s. Born in St. Petersburg in 1891, he was the son of Alexander Pavlovich Chekhov, the talented older brother of the famous playwright Anton Pavlovich Chekhov. After studying acting in St. Petersburg and working with the Maly Theatre, Chekhov studied with Constantin Stanislavsky at the Moscow Art Theatre. Chekhov became the major exponent of Stanislavsky's new acting system at the First Studio of the Moscow Art Theatre, and in 1924 became the head of the Second Moscow Art Theatre. In the 1920s, Chekhov's performances, especially the title characters in *Eric XIV* and *Hamlet,* were highly regarded by the Russian public and established Chekhov as one of the greatest Russian actors of the twentieth century.

After his emigration from the Soviet Union in 1928, Chekhov acted in Germany and France, but was also influential as a director. He directed *Twelfth Night* for the Habima Theatre, which toured the production throughout Europe and England. He also directed a variety of productions, including the opera *Parsifal* in Lithuania and Riga, Latvia, where he subsequently established a theatre school.

Chekhov's performances with the Moscow Art Players, which toured the United States in the 1930s, gained him recognition in this country as a great actor and led to an invitation to lead a theatre studio in Dartington Hall, England. At this studio and later at the Ridgefield Studio in Connecticut, Chekhov established himself as an important director and teacher of his unique system of acting. He taught many British and American actors at these studios and several film actors in Hollywood during the last years of his life. In addition to teaching in Hollywood, he also committed to paper his ideas concerning the art of acting. Hence, as a theorist he left a legacy of an acting system that has been influential in actor training since its appearance in 1953.

There is a well-deserved renascence of interest in Mikhail Chekhov both in the United States and in the Soviet Union. This interest creates a need for comprehensive information about Chekhov. At present there is little readily available information about Chekhov's life and work. Although most theatre people have heard of Mikhail Chekhov, few know much about him, except that he wrote *To the Actor* and is some relation to Anton Chekhov. Works in English by or about Mikhail Chekhov are scarce, and the materials in Russian have been dealt with only tangentially by English-speaking scholars. Even though at his death he left behind many students and disciples, until recently there was no institution to carry on his work and to proliferate his ideas. As a result, there is a danger that the only records of this great man's life and work that will survive will be general histories, giving little understanding of this incredibly complex and interesting artist, and even less insight into the essence of the system of acting he developed.

All translations of Russian material are my own, except where noted. Since this work is aimed at those who are not necessarily Russian scholars, I use the Library of Congress system for transliteration of Russian words as words and bibliographical material, as described in System II of J. Thomas Shaw's *The Transliteration of Modern Russian for English Language Publications.* For personal and place names within the body of the book, I use Shaw's System I.

Of the available works written by Chekhov, *To the Actor on the Technique of Acting,* published in 1953, is the most popular. It is the final result of Chekhov's attempts to record his discoveries about the art of acting in order to pass on his knowledge to other artists. This work is a comprehensive discussion of the art of acting, which evolved from two other works written by Chekhov. The first of these earlier works is an unpublished version of *To the Actor* completed in 1942. Following the advice of Stanislavsky and Rudolf Steiner that it was important for him to record his views about acting, Chekhov wrote this earlier version with the help of Paul Marshall Allen and Deirdre Hurst du Prey. This work is more detailed than the published version but is not readily available. The other version of *To the Actor* is available, but it is written in Russian. Because of his dissatisfaction with the 1942 version, Chekhov rewrote the book himself in Russian and had it published at his own expense. This Russian version, entitled *O tekhnike aktera (On the Technique of Acting),* contains more information on the Anthroposophical influences that were crucial to the formation, if not the practice, of Chekhov's system, and references to the teaching of Rudolf Steiner.

There is another work in English, *To the Director and Playwright,* which was edited by Charles Leonard and published after Chekhov's death. Supposedly, Chekhov had worked on the book with Leonard and would have finished it if he had lived. Much of the main text is an edited transcription of taped lectures that Chekhov gave to the Hollywood Society of Film Actors. Chekhov's notes on Gogol's *Revizor (The Inspector General)* complete the text.

Chekhov's *Lessons for the Professional Actor* is a recent publication which provides insights into Chekhov's ideas about acting and provides a glimpse of how he communicated these ideas to others. Edited by Deirdre Hurst du Prey, this book contains lectures Chekhov delivered to acting classes in New York in 1941.

There are two other works written by Chekhov in Russian. *Put' aktera (The Actor's Path)*, Chekhov's autobiographical account of his early career, was published in 1928. Copies of this book are available, but the only translation I know of is by Boris Uvaroff and part of the personal collection of Deirdre Hurst du Prey. Chekhov also wrote many articles for *Novyi zhurnal,* a Russian emigré journal published in the United States. Five of these articles comprise an unfinished autobiography entitled, *Zhizn' i vstrechi (Life and Encounters)*. There is an English translation of these articles by Julia Kocich, but it is also not readily available. These articles provide fascinating insights into Chekhov's personal life, and my translations of them are used extensively in this book. Other writings for *Novyi zhurnal* consist of articles about acting and the theatre and an interesting set of letters about Christianity and Anthroposophy which Chekhov wrote to a close friend.

There is somewhat more available material written about Chekhov, but few of these works deal with his life and work in a comprehensive way. There are references to Chekhov in several Russian theatre books, such as Slonim's *Russian Theatre from the Empire to the Soviets* and Gorchakov's *The Theatre in Soviet Russia*. Georgette Boner, with whom Chekhov worked in Paris, has translated *To the Actor* into German *(Michael Tschechow: Werkgeheimnisse der Schauspielkunst)* and added a chapter on Chekhov's work and their work together. Although such works provide valuable information about Chekhov, none of them explore his entire life and career in great detail. Pavel Markov's work *Pervaia studiia MXT (First Studio of MAT)* gives valuable information about Chekhov's work at the Moscow Art Theatre's First Studio, but it is available in English only in a translation at the Lincoln Center Library for the Performing Arts.

The only biography of Chekhov at this time is a work entitled *Mikhail Chekhov* by the Russian writer Victor Gromov. This biography was written in Russian in 1970, one year after Chekhov was "restored" to a position of respect by the Soviet Government. Gromov's book is problematic because its political slant distorts the information it provides.

The most comprehensive work on Chekhov at this time is a dissertation written in 1977 by Nancy Anne Kindelan entitled, *The Theatre of Inspiration: An Analysis of the Acting Theories of Michael Chekhov*. This dissertation provides a great service in pulling together a vast amount of information about Chekhov, making it easier for further studies to be made. Chapters in the work include a general historical and artistic background; a discussion of

Chekhov's system of acting; a comparison between the artistic vision of Stanislavsky and that of Chekhov; a discussion of the two Chekhov studios and conclusions about the importance of Chekhov's acting system. There is also an extensive appendix, including lectures that Chekhov delivered at the Chekhov Studio at Dartington Hall, which were recorded by Deirdre Hurst du Prey.

Another source of material for this book comes from the taped lectures of Mikhail Chekhov speaking to the Hollywood Society of Film Actors. The tapes, introduced by John Dehner, were recorded in 1955, the year of Chekhov's death, and broadcast ten years later by KPFK-FM in Los Angeles. Copies of the tapes are available at the Lincoln Center Library for the Performing Arts. These tapes are a wonderful source of information because they provide details of Chekhov's acting system that are not included in his other works. In addition, they are enlightening because in hearing this information from Chekhov himself one gets a clearer impression of the man than is possible through the printed page.

The final sources of evidence for this work come from personal interviews and my observations of persons teaching Chekhov's acting system in studios in New York. Fortunately, there are many former students and colleagues of Mikhail Chekhov who are willing to talk about his life and work. Mala Powers, a successful actress and the executrix of Chekhov's estate, has been very helpful in opening her files to me. She has been particularly helpful in explaining the place of Anthroposophy in Chekhov's life and work.

I have also had the opportunity to speak with the noted actress Beatrice Straight, Chekhov's former student and teacher of his method, who was primarily responsible for the formation of both studios. An accomplished actress in television and film, as well as a noted stage performer, she was able to give insight into the use of Chekhov's method, its strengths and weaknesses.

Deirdre Hurst du Prey, Chekhov's personal secretary for many years, a former student and now a teacher of his method, has also been very kind in providing much information about Chekhov's life and work. She has over three thousand pages of transcribed lectures which Chekhov delivered at Dartington Hall and Ridgefield, Connecticut. In addition to the 1942 version of *To the Actor,* she has translations of *Put' aktera* and *Zhizn' i vstrechi.*

I have also spoken with Georgy Semenovich Zhdanov (George Shdanoff), a Russian actor, director and playwright, who was a close friend and associate of Chekhov for many years. Mr. Zhdanov was with Chekhov during the tenure of both studios, wrote the script for *The Possessed* and has his own theatre studio in Los Angeles.

Ford Rainey, an actor with the Ridgefield Studio, provided much insight into the workings of the Studio. Since he played Sir Toby Belch in *Twelfth Night* and Lear in productions which the Studio toured, he was able to give a detailed account of what it was like to work with Chekhov. John Dehner, the noted television and film actor who worked with Chekhov during the later years of his life, told about the tremendous effect Chekhov had on his career, as well as the careers of many others in Hollywood. Paul Rogers, who played Sir in the Broadway production of Ronald Harwood's *The Dresser,* told of his indebtedness to Mikhail Chekhov. Rogers was discovered by Beatrice Straight and Deirdre Hurst du Prey, who brought him to Chekhov at Dartington Hall, where Rogers received the acting training that has been the basis of his career.

At present there are two acting studios in New York that teach Chekhov's system of acting. The Michael Chekhov Studio was founded by Beatrice Straight in September of 1980 to teach Chekhov's system to young actors and to ensure that this system is properly passed on to future generations. In 1982, I observed a class at the Studio taught by Blair Cutting, who was with the Ridgefield Studio and possessed a certificate from Chekhov as a teacher of Chekhov's system of acting. Mr. Cutting has since died, but his valuable work at the Michael Chekhov Studio has been carried on by teachers such as Felicity Cummings and Elenore Faison, in addition to the teaching of Mrs. Straight and Mrs. du Prey. Because of disagreements about how the system should be taught, another studio, a Michael Chekhov Study Center, headed by Eddie Grove who studied extensively with Chekhov in Los Angeles, also exists. In addition to observing Mr. Grove's class, I was able to speak with him at length about Chekhov's acting system. Although there are strong disagreements between the studios as to how the system should be taught, it is hoped that they both can survive and continue to share with young actors the benefits of seriously studying Chekhov's techniques.

There are many people, in addition to those already mentioned, who have made important contributions to the realization of this book. I would like to thank William Snyder for first introducing me to Chekhov when I was an undergraduate acting student and for his continued guidance, support and friendship. I thank David Heilweil at the University of Connecticut for his information about Chekhov's students at the Ridgefield Studio. The Department of Slavic Languages and Literatures and the Soviet and East European Studies Center at the University of Kansas provided valuable training and a Foreign Language Area Studies fellowship, which greatly aided my research. Gerald Mikkelson, chairperson of Slavic Languages and Literatures, was especially helpful. The Division of Speech and Drama and Department of Theatre at the University of Kansas, particularly William Kuhlke, John Gronbeck-Tedesco, Paul Campbell, Jack Wright, Ron Willis and Bobby Patton, provided a doctoral program of which I am extremely proud. William Kuhlke, my advisor, teacher and friend, first made me aware of the importance of this work and guided it carefully. My friends and colleagues, Alex Boguslawsky, Jem Graves, Kenn Wessel and Mary Dellesaga deserve credit for their help and support during the early drafts of this manuscript. I would also like to thank the Communication and Theatre Arts faculties at Emporia State University for their support during this book's completion.

My mother's unending support is appreciated and my father's inspiration is still with me. Finally, I would like to thank Connie, Elizabeth, Nicholas and Christopher for being the best family ever, for understanding and supporting my work, for loving and caring.

Part One

Background

1

Chekhov's Youth and Religion

The Young Misha

Mikhail Alexandrovich Chekhov begins his autobiographical articles, *Zhizn' i vstrechi (Life and Encounters)* with the following statement: "The first person whom I 'encountered' in life, a man who deeply affected me, was my father. I trembled before him; was amazed at him; was afraid that I would never be able to love him."[1] These articles were written in Chekhov's native language for a Russian emigré audience. He was fifty-three at the time and although he had been fluent in English for many years, he still wrote best in Russian. This was a period in his life when he devoted much energy to writing. He had recently completed the first English version of *To the Actor,* but was currently rewriting it in Russian, because he was dissatisfied with the way in which his ideas were communicated in English.

Of all his "encounters" I find those with his father most interesting, and I feel they indicate the primary influence Alexander Pavlovich Chekhov had on Mikhail's early life. This influence was not always positive. In fact much pain came from their difficult relationship. However, Mikhail's vivid imagination, his interest in philosophy and his ability to understand characters from history are directly attributable to his encounters with his father.

Alexander Pavlovich Chekhov was a journalist, writer, natural scientist, mathematician and philosopher, fluent in many languages. Mikhail's lasting image of his father was of a frighteningly large man with awesome physical, spiritual and mental powers. His father seemed fearless and able to subjugate anyone and anything to his capricious desires. Unfortunately, he had such an individual spirit and disregard for anything ordinary that he was never able to use in any systematic, practical manner his vast knowledge and what Mikhail described as his "tremendous life force." Alexander's other major problem in life was that he was a prodigious alcoholic. This alcoholism caused tremendous tensions in the Chekhov household and placed great burdens on the young Misha (as he was called by those close to him), even though some of the most invigorating encounters between father and son occurred when

Alexander was drunk. Alexander and his younger brother, Anton Pavlovich Chekhov, were very close. Anton once said about him: "Alexander is much more talented than I, but he will perish from hard drinking."[2]

It is difficult to describe Alexander Chekhov's character as anything but extraordinary. He despised any objects that were common. He made his own wall clocks out of wood and decorations such as branches, corks and moss. Huge bottles of water were substituted for weights. He hated the typewriter and refused to use it, because it required the same energy to make a comma as it did to make a letter. In an effort to combat the commonplace world around him, he became obsessed by one scientific experiment after another. The quill pens he used for his many writings came from the expensive, rare breeds of chickens he raised. Instead of providing the normal shelter and food for his chickens, Alexander developed an entire system of living which his chickens were forced to follow. He proclaimed that his chickens must eat and behave according to his rules. He would force feed them or starve them, as he tried to discover the true way a chicken should be fed. He told the roosters which hens they should pursue. He decided that one door of the chicken coop was the entrance and the other was the exit. Any chicken that violated this distinction was chased and threatened. When his wife pointed out to him that many of his chickens died because of his unreasonable demands, he replied that only a certain percentage died and their death benefited scientific research.

Alexander involved the entire household in many of his experiments. It was his son Misha, however, who was his closest and most intimate collaborator in his wild schemes. This meant that Misha had to put away his toys and join in the experiments. For example, once Alexander decided to make linoleum for his study floor.[3] Misha was forced for several days to stir a mixture of old newspapers, water and clay, until the contents resembled linoleum. In spite of the physical pain, fatigue and monotony this work caused, Misha was so afraid of his father that he never protested. When the mixture resembled lineoleum, Alexander put it on the floor of his study, left it for a while and then tore it so that the floor resembled the surface of the moon. He thought that this moon-like floor would create an environment conducive to work. However, Alexander quickly tired of this floor and forced Misha to help him remove the linoleum.

A result of this forced participation in experiments was that in between them Misha would strive to do as quickly as he could whatever would give him satisfaction. He commented that this hurried sense of agitation, of trying to get the most pleasure in the least amount of time, stayed with him for many years. His father's domination made Chekhov a frightened, insecure child who had difficulty relating to other children. Once while playing war with a group of boys, Misha enthusiastically supported his group of soldiers against the enemy. But suddenly, Misha's group turned against him, humiliating and shaming him. This type of experience is not uncommon among children, but because of his insecurities this episode stayed with Chekhov for the rest of his life and furthered his tendency to withdraw into himself.

However, there were positive sides to his relationship with his father. Alexander frequently went on all-night drinking sprees in his study, forcing Misha to be his companion. Misha was amazed that the alcohol never seemed to alter Alexander's mental capacities as these nights produced new and wonderful though sometimes frightening experiences for Misha. They played chess and drew caricatures. In a few strokes, Alexander was able to capture the outward appearance, as well as the inner essence, of a person. As a result, Misha developed a love for caricatures that stayed with him. He drew marvelous make-up sketches for the Ridgefield Studio's production of *King Lear*. His play *Don Quixote* was accompanied by drawings of the characters in various scenes throughout the play. He wrote a fairytale for his wife, Ksenia, which is illustrated wonderfully with caricatured figures.

These recurring nights with his father also provided great stimulation for Misha's developing imagination. In the mysterious atmosphere of the darkening room, Alexander told his son stories about the stars and planets, skillfully picturing them with his voice and gestures. As the night passed, Alexander's behavior grew more bizarre and the atmosphere of the room grew more oppressive. Misha was, at the same time, frightened by and attracted to this atmosphere and the actions of his father. The awareness and use of atmosphere later became an important part of Chekhov's acting system.

As dawn arrived after these long nights, Alexander told Misha about the development of human consciousness. In a clear and coherent manner, he began with the Greeks and guided Misha, step by step, through time, explaining all the major philosophers. Alexander's explanations were so clear that Misha developed images of the people who were the most interesting to him. In his imagination the amusing images of the philosophers appeared, disappeared and at times reminded him of his close friends. As these tales of philosophers were developing Misha's imagination, they were also developing an interest in philosophy, which he pursued intensely in his later life, focusing particularly on Nietzsche and Schopenhauer.

Alexander Chekhov went through long periods of drunkenness, followed by periods of being sober and quite productive as a journalist. When Anton Chekhov, whom he worshiped and loved deeply, died in 1904, Alexander became very distraught and began to drink heavily again. His health grew worse as he travelled and drank without stopping. Without ever displaying a fear of death, he predicted the day that he would die.[4] He died in 1911, the same year that Mikhail, along with Sulerzhitsky and Vakhtangov, started the First Studio of the Moscow Art Theatre.

Mikhail was with his father when he died, and that experience had a strong effect on his feelings about death and how a death scene should be played on stage. For several days and nights, Chekhov watched his father being tortured by nightmarish visions and anger at his own suffering. When he finally died, there was a final convulsion that ran through his face and then a stillness, which seemed to Mikhail as an unresolved musical chord. This stillness was an unexpected element, which he incorporated into the deaths of characters he played on stage. In portraying the deaths of Ivan the Terrible, Erik XIV and Hamlet, Chekhov expressed the peace experienced by these characters as they died. Chekhov interpreted this peace as representing the characters' souls leaving this world and entering another world.[5] When Chekhov directed Ford Rainey in the role of King Lear at the Ridgefield Studio, it was very important to Chekhov that Rainey work on capturing what Chekhov saw as the spiritual death and then rebirth of Lear at the end of the play.[6]

Chekhov spoke with a different emphasis about portraying death on stage in the *New World Telegram* of March 2, 1935. The same concept is implicit but he focuses on the use of tempo to express the slowing down process of death. Speaking about his father's death, he said:

> It was the first time I had seen death at close quarters. Later I realized how falsely actors portray death upon the stage. Rendering, as they believe, a faithful picture, they pay too much attention to the physiological processes. The more accurately the physical torments of the dying are portrayed, the farther is it removed from the picture of death as it should appear in art. Death upon the stage should be shown as a slowing down and the gradual disappearance of the sense of time.[7]

Chekhov was very close to his mother even though her effect on his professional work did not seem to be as great as the influence Alexander had upon him. Her influence was more personal than professional. Chekhov's mother was very protective of him, and she was a recluse, never wanting to leave the house. As a result, she wanted her Misha always to stay with her. Whether it was intentional or not, she instilled a fear in him that if he left the house, something tragic might happen to her.[8]

Learned fears of this type, added to the neurosis caused by his father's actions, resulted in periods of mental instability for Mikhail Chekhov. His first wife divorced him in 1918 during a period of extreme depression and paranoia brought on by difficulties he was having with the new Soviet government and by the recent death of his mother. A few years later, after he married his second wife Ksenia, he became a recluse within his own house, refusing to go out and refusing to work. Chekhov was able to overcome both of these difficult periods with the help of psychiatrists and hypnosis.

Anthroposophy

When one begins to talk about the religious aspects of Mikhail Chekhov's life and work, there is a danger of giving Anthroposophy an improper emphasis. It should be made clear that he detested the title "mystic" which the Bolsheviks used against him. Many of the people who were close to him do not even like to talk about Chekhov as an Anthroposophist. There seems to be a concern on the part of Chekhov's students that Anthroposophy will get too much emphasis or the wrong kind of emphasis, and, as a result, the idea of Chekhov as "mystic" will be strengthened. However, if one is to understand fully what Chekhov was like as a human being, then it is crucial to examine both his Christianity and his Anthroposophy, the spiritual science that became an important part of his religious life.

Mala Powers Miller, an Anthroposophist and close friend of Mikhail and Ksenia Chekhov, insists that one cannot "separate Chekhov and his performances from his Christianity."[9] This Christianity is based on Russian Orthodoxy but is interpreted through the Christology, or spiritual science, developed by Rudolf Steiner and called Anthroposophy. Chekhov came upon Anthroposophy almost by chance. He often looked into different religions, searching for something that would be meaningful for himself and his art. He was a strong believer in yoga and felt that there was something in the practice of yoga that would be of great use to the actor. He experimented with ways to use it in rehearsals and performances. Since he was very much interested in Nietzsche, Schopenhauer and other philosophers, he also looked constantly for new philosophical ideas and new books by philosophers with whom he was not familiar.

Chekhov related what happened one day on a Moscow street:

> Once, going past a window of the "Writer's Book Shop," my gaze fell, by chance, on a title of a book: *Knowledge of the Higher Worlds and Its Attainment,* by Rudolf Steiner. I smiled ironically. "If one could really know *how* to reach that knowledge, then probably it would already be achieved and it would make no sense for the author to publish his book."[10]

However, Chekhov bought the book, read it, and put it aside. About the same time his interest in yoga had brought Chekhov into contact with the doctrine of Theosophy and he began to meet with several members of the Theosophical Society in Moscow. Theosophy had its roots in *Isis Unveiled* and *Secret Doctrine,* the principle works of Helena Petrovna Blavatsky (1831–91), a Russian clairvoyant.[11] Rudolf Steiner (1861–1925), another clairvoyant, had joined the Theosophical Society because it was a group which allowed him to speak with people who had similar experiences. Steiner later left the

Theosophical Society because of disagreements about Christianity and developed his own brand of spiritual science which he called Anthroposophy.[12]

As Chekhov continued to learn about Theosophy, he became interested in clairvoyance. He visited many of the "secret" societies in Moscow at the time and met with some very unusual characters. One woman with an "otherworldly stare" persuaded him to go with her to a spiritual seance. The seance, as Chekhov describes it, was more comical than spiritual and he developed strong suspicions that this woman had connections with the G.P.U., now known as the K.G.B.[13] It was at this time that the authorities began to label Chekhov a "mystic," as they were preparing for his eventual arrest.

As he studied Theosophy, Chekhov was confused by its connection to orientalism, and it seemed to him that Theosophy underestimated the significance of Christ and the Mystery of Golgotha. Still searching for answers to his questions, he went to two priests, whom he identifies only as Father Aleksey and Father Sergey. Father Sergey answered many of his questions about Christianity, but the priest's devotion to Orthodox dogma left some of his questions still unanswered. As a result, Chekhov went back to Steiner's *Knowledge of the Higher Worlds and Its Attainment* and this time the book really struck him. Explaining the effect the book had on him at the time, Chekhov states:

> There was no "secret," no "mysticism," or desire to make an impression in his [Steiner's] discourse. The simple, clear, scientific style makes simple and clear those facts which were objects of the author's discourse. That which is inaccessible to the sensual perceptions became accessible as a result. I read R. Steiner's whole series of books and this careful reading gave me answers to the questions troubling me then. I learned, for example, that the spiritual world with its Essences develops and changes just as the world of the physical with its essences. *History* happens not only on Earth. The spiritual world in the time of ancient India was different from now, and holding on to the old, timidly shutting one's eyes to the new which arrives from the spiritual world, means to condemn one's self to spiritual atavism.... The spiritual world is "secret" only for him who does not want to apply sufficient effort in order to penetrate it. The first and fundamental exercise offered by R. Steiner leads to the ability of logical-clarity, active thinking. Without this ability, the beginning clairvoyant can fall prey to illusion and instead of the spiritual world, can plunge into the sphere of the fantastic and self-deception.[14]

Hence, after a long period of searching, Chekhov found that Anthroposophy satisfactorily answered his religious questions and fit his ideas about Christianity. He was persuaded to follow the teachings of Steiner, because he was convinced that Christ is at the center of everything about which Steiner speaks. Chekhov saw Anthroposophy as the contemporary form of Christianity. He sums up the personal importance the discovery of

Anthroposophy had for him by saying, "This, my 'encounter' with Anthroposophy, was the happiest period of my life."[15]

Anthroposophy has two main parts: it is a world conception and a spiritual science.[16] This world conception comes from empirical knowledge and from the individual, clairvoyant research of Rudolf Steiner. It is based on the belief that human beings possess the power to see and communicate consciously with the spiritual world. It assumes that within every person there exist certain facilities, and when these facilities are trained and awakened, the limits of knowledge disappear, little by little.

As a spiritual science, Anthroposophy asserts that visions come to people as experiences which are unbidden. Initiation is

> a very conscious path where a man has to transcend his usual physical position in the world and be able consciously to work with other organs of perception that before training slumber within him.... There are actually three stages: imagination, inspiration and intuition. Intuition is the highest.[17]

As a practicing Anthroposophist, Mikhail Chekhov was involved with Anthroposophy both as a world conception and as a spiritual science. He was also a believer in reincarnation, a key Anthroposophical concept.

Rudolf Steiner was very much interested in the arts, and his ideas about eurythmy and speech had a direct effect on Chekhov's system of acting. Briefly, eurythmy is an art that attempts to neutralize the inhibiting power of intellect. Feeling that the intellect is the enemy of all true art, eurythmy aims to make visible the feelings that lie within a particular movement. Steiner felt the character of a movement should originate in the artist's soul, not in the intellect. Eurythmy is "visible speech" or "visible song." Under the guidance of Steiner's wife, Marie Steiner, eurythmy developed in three directions: as stage art, as an educational aid in schools, and as a therapeutic method.[18] Eurythmy was used by Chekhov as a training technique in his studios and presumably was the impetus for his development of psychological gesture.

Steiner's ideas about speech training also were used by Chekhov in his teaching of actors. Steiner commented:

> It is rarely that everyday speech becomes raised to the level of art. We are almost entirely bereft of feeling for the beauty of speech, still more bereft of feeling for speech that is in character.... People nowadays often consider artistic speaking to be misguided idealism. This would never have happened if people had been more aware of the possibility of developing speech as an art.[19]

With these ideas in mind, Steiner and his wife began offering speech formation and drama courses with the aim of raising these skills to the level of true art.

Their methods are explained in a book entitled *Speech and Drama,* which is an anthology of lectures that Steiner gave in the Section for the Arts of Speech and Music at the School of Spiritual Science in the Goetheanum in Dornach, Switzerland.

There is another strong connection between Anthroposophy and Chekhov's system of acting which involves the concept of the "higher I." In *To the Actor,* Chekhov states that the emotions, voice and body constitute the "building material" from which the actor's higher self, the real artist in every actor, creates a character. This higher, creative self is called the "higher I."[20] Chekhov states:

> The true creative state of an actor-artist is governed by a threefold functioning of his consciousness: the higher self inspires his acting and grants him genuinely creative feelings; the lower self serves as the commonsense restraining force; the illusory "soul" of the character becomes the focal point of the higher self's creative impulses.[21]

The "higher I" also connects the performer with the audience, allowing the performer to be aware of the audience's experiences, enthusiasm, excitement and disappointments.

While explaining his beliefs about Christianity in a letter to a close friend, Chekhov uses the same term, "higher I" ("vysshii ia"). According to Chekhov, Christ enters into a person as this person's "higher I." When one talks about his "higher I," he uses the term in the sense of "Christ in me." Explaining this concept to his friend, Chekhov states:

> When (and since) Christ comes into man as "I," this "I," while remaining Christ, becomes at the same time man. How is this possible? God, Christ, Gives Up Himself *without residue.* His sacrifice is *absolute.* Separating out in the capacity of the "I" part of His Essence and having transferred it to man, He speaks, as it were, to this part of Himself: "Now live and develop independently. Become an *individual* man, into which I have placed Myself. I give you freedom." This mystery of the "transformation" of God in man, this purely spiritual event, is wonderfully expressed in Christianity with the words: The Birth of the Christ-Child in the soul of man.[22]

This is an interesting link between religion and the art of acting because it implies that the actor's true creative state is a higher level of consciousness in which dwells Christ, God in man. Hence, as Mikhail Chekhov explains it, true creative acting is elevated to a plane of existence that includes the spirit of Christ. Chekhov was an extremely religious man whose art was infused with his religious beliefs.

This concept of the "higher I" also seems to have roots in the Eastern Orthodox religious tradition of Hesychasm. Hesychasm is "Eastern Christianity's ancient tradition of contemplative monasticism."[23] In the thirteenth century, Hesychasm was a flourishing movement among Eastern Orthodox monks. When it ceased to be an organized movement in the fourteenth century, it continued as a technique of monastic prayer. This technique involved standing or sitting motionless, with head bowed, holding one's breath and reciting the Jesus prayer. The Hesychasts aimed at inner peace through this technique (the Greek work *Hesychia* means silence), but they also aimed at reaching a higher form of consciousness in which they would become one with Christ. In this prayerful state, monks would often experience a vision which was not a product of their imagination but a theopany, a manifestation of God.[24]

To my knowledge, Chekhov never refers directly to Hesychasm as the basis for his concept of the "higher I," but the similarities seem too striking to be coincidental. Chekhov was originally an Eastern Orthodox Christian and, as I discussed earlier, his father gave him long lectures on the history of religion. His connection to hesychasm is strengthened by his visit to the Optina Pustyn' Monastery not long before he left the Soviet Union. In *Life and Encounters* Chekhov records a lengthy visit with Nektary, an elder of this monastery, and says that this encounter had a strong impact on his life and work.[25]

Chekhov was a complex man whose strong beliefs in the spiritual world are not easily categorized. These beliefs, however, make him all the more interesting and encourage us to find connecting links from his personal life to his professional accomplishments. Chekhov's mind was sharp and inquisitive, even when he wrestled with the fears he learned in childhood and during periods of mental instability. His imagination and creativity seemed to be limitless. In this first chapter, we have examined the effects of his childhood and Anthroposophy on his professional work. Using this information as a base, we will next examine the major points of Chekhov's fascinating acting career.

2

Chekhov as a Young Actor

Chekhov's interest in acting began at an early age. At his home, he put on elaborate, improvised productions for his mother and nanny. He performed tragedy and comedy for them, changing costumes to indicate the differences in tragic and comic mood. His mother and nanny were an attentive audience for this energetic child-actor, even though the nanny seldom understood the ideas behind what Misha was doing.[1] Chekhov's enthusiasm for acting grew and led him to A. S. Suvorin's Dramatic School in 1909. Here, at the age of eighteen, he began to study his craft.[2]

After a year at this school, B. Glagolin brought Chekhov to the Maly Theatre where he appeared in his first professional production, *Tsar Fyodor Ioannovich* by Alexey Tolstoy. Chekhov stayed at the Maly from 1910–12 and then auditioned for the Moscow Art Theatre.[3] It was Olga Knipper, wife of Anton Chekhov, who brought Misha to audition for Stanislavsky. Describing this important event in his career, Chekhov said, "What a scene! He [Stanislavsky] asked me to read some lines and my collar burst. And then, to reassure me, he said, 'We are honored to have the nephew of the great Chekhov with the company.' I was terrified. Yet he gave me my chance."[4]

Chekhov became a star pupil of Stanislavsky's new acting system. Although Chekhov developed a system of acting that was very different from what Stanislavsky taught him, he highly regarded Stanislavsky's methods. However, Chekhov found Stanislavsky's insistence on being true to life limiting, and so he explored the uses of imagination and theatricality that he learned from Meyerhold and Vakhtangov. Chekhov's conception of character was quite different from Stanislavsky's. Chekhov disagreed with Stanislavsky's emphasis on the actor's ego, and instead preferred an emphasis on the character's ego. For Stanislavsky, if an actor played a character whose child was ill, the actor imagined his own child ill and responded with truthful emotions. For Chekhov, the actor's focus would be on the character of the father, to study objectively the father's emotions, movements and facial expressions, resulting in an artistic creation that expressed the playwright's conception. Regarding this difference, Chekhov stated:

The difference is that with Stanislavsky's method, the character's child becomes the actor's focal point, since the actor must see only the things seen by the character residing within him. With mine, the *character* becomes the focal point, which after all is the actor's true objective, and through the character the actor is able to feel so much more of what the father feels for the child than he could possibly be capable of on his own, by doing it *for* the father, as it were.

That was the gist of what we discussed—the supremacy of the character's ego (mine) against the actor's ego (Stanislavsky's)—and I must confess that neither of us convinced the other.[5]

In spite of their disagreements, Chekhov acknowledged his indebtedness to Stanislavsky and the importance of Stanislavsky's contributions to the theatre. Chekhov said:

his [Stanislavsky's] pioneering achievements on his own and in collaboration with his coworkers must be acknowledged as the first monumental contributions to the art of the theatre in the past and present centuries. Others are said to have surpassed and even by-passed him but he, together with Nemirovich-Danchenko, was the first to break the land that opened up the new fields which all of us later tilled in our own distinctive ways.[6]

Stanislavsky greatly admired Chekhov's talent and creative individuality. During rehearsals for the Moscow Art Theatre production of *The Inspector General* in 1922, Stanislavsky watched Chekhov from the auditorium. His eyes were glued to the stage and he was afraid to move or make the slightest sound for fear of disturbing Chekhov's creativity.[7]

Stanislavsky took *The Inspector General* out of its historical period and emphasized the truth of Gogol's satire through a forceful molding of the characters. This freed Chekhov to create a bold and grotesque Khlestakov that was a symbol of emptiness and evil. His grotesque characterization combined a bold use of gesture and intonations with a deep psychological refinement. Audiences were as transfixed by Chekhov's Khlestakov in performance as Stanislavsky was in rehearsal. Slonim states, "The spiritual tension and depth of this interpretation were carried over to the spectators with such hypnotic power that they remained spellbound and shivering."[8] Stanislavsky once told a group of students, "Study the system of Misha Chekhov. Everything that I teach you is contained in his actor's individuality."[9]

For several years before Chekhov joined the Moscow Art Theatre, Stanislavsky experimented with the idea of establishing workshops as vehicles for experimentation. He had experimented with the symbolist plays of Andreyev and Maeterlinck at the Moscow Art Theatre but he was not satisfied with the results. His newly developing system of acting was more suited to realistic works but he felt that other forms should be explored. In 1905, Stanislavsky established a studio under the direction of Vsevolod

Meyerhold with the purpose of producing various types of plays that did not fit into the repertory of the Moscow Art Theatre.[10] However, Meyerhold's experiments went in directions that Stanislavsky did not intend. Stanislavsky was interested in the importance of the actor and thought the Studio would be a place to explore his new acting system. Meyerhold became concerned with developing productions which Stanislavsky felt subordinated the actor and emphasized the importance of the aesthetic whole. Meyerhold was becoming a dictatorial director whose idea of aesthetic whole was the product of his vivid imagination and his newly formed idea of a "spiritual theatre." Meyerhold attempted, "to stage the unreal, to render life as perceived in fantasy and visions."[11] These ideas caused a split between Meyerhold and Stanislavsky. The Studio was discontinued. Meyerhold went to work at Vera Komissarzhevskaya's theatre and Stanislavsky continued to look for the proper workshop to complement the work done at the Moscow Art Theatre.

As Stanislavsky's new system of acting began to take shape, he strengthened his efforts to find a way to test and refine his ideas. Many of the older actors at the Moscow Art Theatre were supportive of Stanislavsky's efforts but hesitant to apply this new system to their own work. In an effort to further develop and test his acting system, Stanislavsky sent Leopold Sulerzhitsky, one of his most talented disciples, to teach Stanislavsky's acting theories to students in the private Adashev School in Moscow. In 1911, the year before Chekhov joined the Moscow Art Theatre, Stanislavsky established the First Studio of the Moscow Art Theatre with Sulerzhitsky as head.[12]

Leopold Sulerzhitsky had begun working at the Moscow Art Theatre as a stage hand but soon became one of Stanislavsky's most talented and ardent followers. He had a great love for humanity and was an idealist who sought inspiration for his creative work through communion with nature, simplicity of living and active love.[13] His conception of theatre as a means of bringing people together and provoking in them genuine emotions meshed well with Stanislavsky's system and the two men became close personal friends. The First Studio accomplished Stanislavsky's objectives and provided the environment for Chekhov to develop his talents under the guidance of Sulerzhitsky and Evgeny Vakhtangov, who joined the First Studio after having studied under Sulerzhitsky at the Adashev School.

Sulerzhitsky worked diligently with the young actors of the Studio, teaching and testing Stanislavsky's acting system. Both men felt that a key to this Studio training was to break down the traditional separation between actor and audience. The Studio's theatre seated between one hundred and one hundred fifty spectators. The stage was not separated from the rows of seats and the traditional footlights were eliminated. For Stanislavsky this theatre created an intimacy that made the audience not just spectators but involved witnesses to the life created on stage. Stanislavsky felt that this intimacy allowed the actors to act without straining and to develop their voices and gestures. Once these skills were strengthened, the actor would then be able to perform on a larger stage. [14] For Sulerzhitsky, this intimacy strengthened the union between actor and audience, making the audience an active part of the creative process. He felt that traditional theatres, with footlights and physical distance between actor and audience, kept the vital reactions of the audience from reaching the actor. "This is one of the reasons why studios are formed: the stage artist, the artist who creates in public isolation, needs the sense of an audience, for in the presence of a third author—the public—one can grow, develop and perfect oneself." [15]

Sulerzhitsky developed three goals for the First Studio: (1) the development of the psychology of creative acting, (2) making the actor *self-conscious*, and (3) bringing the actor and author close together. [16] The Studio differed from the Moscow Art Theatre in that all settings and properties were simplified and the actors did almost all of the work, which at the Art Theatre was reserved for technical theatre specialists. For example, Mikhail Chekhov and Sulerzhitsky made all of the toys used in the 1914 production of *The Cricket on the Hearth*. Sulerzhitsky was drawn toward an unassuming conventionality of settings at the First Studio, which put little emphasis on spectacle and more emphasis on the actor creating the type of atmosphere required by the play. [17]

Sulerzhitsky always demanded from his actors a fundamental quality of humaneness that would permeate any character being played. Regardless of how funny, awkward or odd a character became, his compassionate, modest inner qualities and naive feelings always showed through. He vacillated between a contemplation of the unaffected and elementary and a preoccupation with the character's deepest psychological problems. For him, an understanding of human nature, with all its virtues and faults, in its simplicity and complexity, was crucial to the creative expression of the actor.

At the First Studio Chekhov's acting talents matured. What he learned from Sulerzhitsky and Stanislavsky was the basis for his development as an actor. However, Evgeny Vakhtangov, [18] through his approach to theatre as a synthesis of the features of both Stanislavsky and Meyerhold, had an even greater impact on Chekhov.

Vakhtangov termed his synthesis of Stanislavsky and Meyerhold "fantastic realism." [19] According to this concept, an actor needed inner justification based on true emotions, but the externals were an exaggerated reflection of the inner realities which at times became grotesque but maintained a connection with reality. The result was a theatricalism that went beyond the limits of naturalism, a literal imitation of life, and realism, a selected reflection of reality, to create forms that were not mere imitations but products of the director's imagination. As a result, theatrical truth became more important than what was true to life. Vakhtangov stated:

> In the theatre there should be neither naturalism nor realism, but there should be fantastic realism. Properly devised theatrical methods make the author come alive on the stage. The methods can be learned, but the form must be created, constructed through one's imagination. That is why I call it fantastic realism. Fantastic realism exists; it should exist now in every art.[20]

Vakhtangov expressed his ideas through his production of Ibsen's *Rosmersholm* at the First Studio in 1918 and in Strindberg's *Erik XIV* in 1921. *Erik XIV* was a triumph for Vakhtangov's methods and "for the first time, the great talent of Mikhail Chekhov [as Erik] was presented in all its creative maturity."[21] This production made use of cubism and realism. The ordinary people of the play were shown realistically in a realistic environment, but the royal characters, in their gestures, intonations, makeup and costumes, were grotesquely tragic in the style of cubism.[22]

In 1922 Vakhtangov produced Carlo Gozzi's *Princess Turandot* at the Third Studio, later renamed the Vakhtangov Theatre, giving full of expression to his concept of fantastic realism.[23] Vakhtangov turned Gozzi's play about the cruel Princess into a joyful, theatrical celebration, using characters of the *commedia dell'arte* and an abundance of theatrical tricks and devices. Four stock *commedia* characters introduced the play as the other actors, in evening dress, talked and joked with the audience. Then these actors began to transform their evening dress into costumes, using various materials located on the stage. A scarf became a beard; a towel became a turban; a shawl was transformed into a dress. This was all done to the music of the orchestra which included kazoos and cigarette paper and combs among its instruments. The entire production had the feeling of spontaneous improvisation but was carefully planned and worked out to the minutest detail. The audience never forgot that it was in a theatre, and the actors carefully balanced reality and theatricality. During one scene, an actor came down stage and told the audience a sad story. He was crying real tears in the best tradition of Stanislavsky's inner belief, when another actor entered with a cup, caught the tears, showed them to the audience and applauded the other actor for his masterful technique.

Princess Turandot was Vakhtangov's final production. He was dying of cancer and too sick to see a performance of the play. Confined to his bed, Vakhtangov asked Stanislavsky to attend the final dress rehearsal. After the rehearsal, Stanislavsky called Vakhtangov and ecstatically congratulated him for the artistic accomplishments of the production.[24] This production was also a commercial success and is still considered a masterful achievement of one of Russia's most influential directors. With Vakhtangov's death in 1922, Mikhail

Chekhov took over the leadership of the First Studio. In 1924 it was renamed the Second Moscow Art Theatre, and Chekhov remained its leader until his emigration in 1928.

Sulerzhitsky and Vakhtangov were the directorial leaders of the First Studio, but Mikhail Chekhov provided the leadership and inspiration for the actors of the Studio. Because of their friendship and close artistic collaboration, it is difficult to tell whether Vakhtangov influenced Chekhov or Chekhov influenced Vakhtangov.[25] However, Chekhov's individual accomplishments were crucial to the success of the First Studio.

> He [Chekhov] was one of the first participants and organizers. Beginning with *The Shipwreck of "Hope"* and ending with *Erik XIV* and *The Archangel Michael,* he was always among its builders. All his major roles were played at the Studio and only his Khlestakov was played at the Moscow Art Theatre itself. His actor's path is the path of the Studio.[26]

Of the roles Chekhov performed at the First Studio and Second Moscow Art Theatre, his Erik XIV and Hamlet are generally considered to be his best. Chekhov took the notion of eliciting compassion for characters, which he learned from Sulerzhitsky, and applied it to his portrayal of Erik. Especially with villainous characters, Chekhov sought to understand why they acted as they did, and as a result, created a performance which touched the audience's sympathies, regardless of the character's evil deeds. By penetrating the psychological core of the villainous Erik, Chekhov showed him as a man possessed by an idea which led to his tragic fate. At the same time, he made clear positive sides of this villain, resulting in a portrayal that was complex and stirring.

Chekhov loved his villains for their shortcomings as well as their virtues, and as a result avoided portrayals that were cold or unsympathetic.[27] He built his tragic characters according to contrasts so that joy and understanding pervaded the tragic in spite of the pessimism of the characters being played. Commenting on Chekhov's Erik, Gorchakov states:

> For the first time this actor [Chekhov] showed the enormous range of his skills. In his intonations, in his outcry suddenly erupting from a whisper, in his hasty and impetuous motions, in his incredibly dynamic transition from shading to shading, he unveiled the character of a person torn apart by contradictions.[28]

Alexander Chekhov's influence on his son was revealed in *Erik XIV.* Chekhov seemed to have captured Erik in the same way his father captured the essence of people in his caricature drawings.

> For his interpretation of the tragic quality in Erik, Chekhov found an accentuated and articulate form. The performance was marked by a cold and rigorous graphic quality. It seemed that this quality was expressed by every movement, gesture; the posture of his body in space; the hand which darted out and remained suspended in the air; the hopeless

melancholic gaze of the morbidly wide-opened eyes upon the elongated, wondering face; the thin hands and feet slipping out from the silver garments; the sudden uplifts and plungings of the timid and bold movements. It seemed that his whole bearing could be put on paper and fixated in the form of a clear drawing.[29]

As Alexander Chekhov's caricatures expressed the outward appearance and inner being of a person, Mikhail Chekhov developed an artistic physical form that expressed the inner essence of Erik.

Chekhov's *Hamlet,* produced during the Second Moscow Art Theatre's 1924–25 season, was described as the most outstanding presentation of the Russian theatre during this period.[30] Instead of carefully articulating an external form, Chekhov focused more keenly on the psychological motivations that caused Hamlet to act. In the performance, he made clear Hamlet's personal suffering brought about by the struggle to be liberated from the evil that surrounded him. Chekhov felt that the tragedy of Hamlet was the result of the character's necessity to act against the evil that enveloped him. In spite of Hamlet's hatred of murder, he committed it, fully aware of the moral law being broken. In Chekhov's performance the ethical problems of the character were not handled metaphysically through rationalizations but were shown concretely through Hamlet's actions. Instead of being weak and lacking will, Chekhov's Hamlet was infused with an eagerness for action which led to the character's pain and suffering.[31] Russian audiences responded well to this portrait of a man's sufferings because human suffering was a very real thing to them. The performance solidified Chekhov's position as one of the leading actors of his time and was an important step in the development of his talents. Markov comments:

He arrived at a universal character who was at the same time real and endowed with an active will. . . . Hamlet explains a great deal of the early Chekhov: the morbid sensitiveness of his former heroes, the double interweaving of laughter and suffering, . . . the exaggerated sharpness of his scenic forms. In *Hamlet* Chekhov appeared as one who had found his focal center, who had found his inner content.[32]

It is important to note that Markov saw Chekhov's personal life as a reflection of Hamlet's character. Chekhov lived in the terribly difficult times of the Russian revolution and overcame the gloom around him through the concentrated force of his personal will.

He carried through those years the best there was in the Russian theatre. He vindicated this art by a current which flowed altogether beyond the realm of aesthetics. He strengthened it in the last years. That is how Chekhov echoed the actualities of modern life.[33]

Even though Chekhov's *Hamlet* received high audience acclaim and won him the title of Honored Artist of the R.S.F.S.R.,[34] the performance intensified his difficulties with the Communist authorities who felt his portrayal of Hamlet was too depressing and did nothing to further the Communist cause.[35] The Second Moscow Art Theatre was already frowned upon by the Communists because it had not produced a revolutionary play. The theatre was tolerated for a while by the government because of its association with the Moscow Art Theatre and because of the excellence of its productions.

However, as the Bolsheviks realized they needed theatre only as a propaganda tool, all the great innovative theatres came under severe attack. The full-scale attack on these theatres began in 1927. The Moscow Art Theatre, which had earlier been praised by the Bolsheviks as the classical theatre for Soviet Socialist realism, was severely attacked in the decade following 1927 and stamped as the "naturalistic and impressionistic romanticism of the disillusioned, Russian, middle-class intellectuals."[36] Meyerhold, who was regarded earlier as the primary leader of the Soviet theatre, was severely attacked as being linked to mystical and symbolist experiments. The Kamerny Theatre was branded as partisan to the rotting bourgeoisie, and Tairov, its director, was labeled a pitiful eclectic.

Anatoly Lunacharsky, who had earlier defended the Moscow Art Theatre, wrote in 1938 that all the studios of the Moscow Art Theatre, "lacked not only any kind of social or philosophical ideology, but even an ideology of the theatre."[37] The authorities were also disturbed by the intangible power Chekhov had over those who saw him perform. In his production of *Hamlet,* Chekhov chose not to have anyone or anything actually appear as the ghost of King Hamlet. He chose instead to project the existence of the ghost solely through his own imagination and energy. Chekhov was so successful that audiences swore they could see something which was not there.[38] Hence, Chekhov was labeled a "mystic" and a propaganda campaign was started to discredit him.

As this campaign intensified, Chekhov's theatre was called "sick," "alien" and "reactionary." Chekhov himself was pronounced, "a 'sick actor' who spurted a mystical infection toward the entire Soviet theatre. His best role—Hamlet—was a mystical nightmare alien to the materialistic cognition held by the toiling masses."[39] Chekhov felt spies were placed among his company of actors, and he was under constant surveillance.

Adding to Chekhov's problems, the company of the Second Moscow Art Theatre became divided between those who considered themselves good Marxists, led by Alexey Diky, and those who were idealists, like Chekhov. In 1927 Diky, Vakhtangov's former student, organized a group of sixteen people to leave the Theatre and publicly condemn Chekhov's methods.[40] It is not clear how much of this discord was political in nature and how much was artistic. Chekhov was justified in thinking there were persons in his theatre who were reporting his activities to the G.P.U. One might suspect that his paranoia was creating an unknown enemy among his ranks who was out to destroy him. However, the propaganda campaign against him was sufficient to legitimize his suspicions.

In addition to the political issue, there were also conflicts created by Chekhov's rehearsal techniques. He had been experimenting freely since taking over the Second Moscow Art Theatre, and some of these experiments were met with resistance from the acting company. While rehearsing *Hamlet*, for example, Chekhov had actors juggling balls in the air while they spoke their lines in an effort to physicalize Shakespeare's language. He also pushed them to find archetypes, or ideal images, which would lead them to the character's ego, instead of building on their own personalities or stereotypes suggested by the playwright.[41] Chekhov's innovative methods had become too intangible and idealistic for many of his actors.

After this dissension in his theatre, Chekhov knew that he must eventually leave Russia or face certain arrest. He waited as long as he could. When he learned from a government official, who was also his friend, that he was about to be apprehended, Chekhov and his wife Ksenia Karlovna arranged to leave Russia on a "vacation." In 1928 on the evening before he was to be arrested, the Chekhovs gathered a few personal belongings, departed their homeland and never returned.

The seven-year period from 1928 to 1935 was one of difficult transition for Mikhail Chekhov. He went first to Berlin with the intention of recreating his performance of Hamlet.[42] Having already memorized the first act in German and with an expensive German-language volume of *Hamlet* at his side, he went to see a German entrepreneur, who was known for producing quality productions. This entrepreneur greeted Chekhov kindly with lavish compliments but would not even consider the possibility of Chekhov performing Hamlet. Instead, he had plans for Chekhov to perform in a cabaret. He commented, "I will make out of you the second Grok [a famous Swiss Clown]."[43] This entrepreneur was working for Max Reinhardt and was similar to our modern agent. Chekhov described this man as an entrepreneur to emphasize his obsession with making money. He offered Chekhov a year's contract, giving a set salary per month and giving himself the right to sell Chekhov as he wished to stage productions or films. Chekhov was shocked by the offer. All of his artistic ideals seemed to be compromised by this entrepreneur's offer. Chekhov tried to protest but his employer was adamant, saying that the public would pay to see a cabaret but they had no interest in *Hamlet* at this time.

Chekhov's debut as a clown was to be as the character Skid in *Artisten*, a production directed by Max Reinhardt. Chekhov soon met with Reinhardt who explained the role to Chekhov and reassured him that even though the public did not want to see *Hamlet* now, the classics would again be popular.

Chekhov was to perform in Vienna, and he went there immediately to work on his German pronunciation with Reinhardt's assistant and to learn the clown tricks required. This preparation period proved to be very difficult for Chekhov. Reinhardt's assistant was harsh and dictatorial in correcting Chekhov's pronunciation and intonations. At the same time, Chekhov's regular acrobatic lessons were strenuous and exhausting.

In spite of the problems Chekhov experienced during the preparation of *Artisten,* his performance in the play brought him high praise from the public and Reinhardt.[44] More importantly, it provided Chekhov the realization of a very important aspect of his acting technique. He had been trying for several years to order his ideas about acting into a systematic approach. He was especially interested in the problem of achieving and using inspiration. Ironically, his work on he clown, Skid, brought Chekhov's ideas about inspiration into focus, and was a pivotal point in the formation of Chekhov's acting system.

During a performance of a long monologue in the third act of the play, Chekhov was surprised to find that his consciousness was separated from that of the character.[45] He was both performing the character and observing it from the outside. He was personally at ease as the character was experiencing pain. The audience was spellbound and the other actors were relating to Chekhov more completely than they had in rehearsals. As one part of Chekhov's consciousness watched and gave commands to the character, another part of his consciousness performed as the character. He had complete control over the performance, but his consciousness was also in the audience and in each of his fellow actors. This came as a surprise to Chekhov. He had not rehearsed the role this way. As a result of this split consciousness, however, both Chekhov's and Skid's entire beings were filled with an incredible power that filled the theatre.

This experience validated Chekhov's ideas about inspiration by relating it to the concept of "higher I" discussed in chapter 1. Chekhov's religion and art merged here to crystalize an important part of his approach to acting. In *Life and Encounters,* Chekhov explained that in every creative individual there exists the "higher I" and "lower I" that combat each other to rule the consciousness of the individual.[46] The "lower I," involved with passions and ego, usually dominates in everyday life, but the "higher I" should rule during the artistic process. As with the performance of Skid, the "higher I" should provide the inspiration that is expressed through the "lower I" as the performer. Hence, the actor directs the feelings of the character but personally maintains a certain detachment from these feelings. This is another example of the difference between Chekhov and Stanislavsky discussed earlier. By establishing a character's ego through inspiration, one avoids the issue of

Stanislavsky's actor's ego which requires the actor to experience fully the emotions experienced by the character. Chekhov stated:

> Bad actors are proud that they are sometimes able to "feel" something on stage; that they lose themselves! These actors break furniture, twist their partners' hands and strangle their lovers as they are performing. These actors who "experience feelings," very often lapse into hysterics behind the scenes. [47]

Chekhov's ideas about acting began to solidify at this point in his career, as he began to find keys to expressing the processes he followed as an actor. His notions of how an actor should approach a part were by no means set in stone at this point, and these notions would continue to evolve throughout his lifetime. This performance of Skid was significant, however, because it provided a basis upon which Chekhov would build. Perhaps the entrepreneur did Chekhov a favor by not allowing him to perform Hamlet in Germany, in spite of how difficult this experience was. Chekhov viewed Skid initially as a paltry test of endurance, lacking in artistic merit. He was fighting for survival in a world concerned as much with commercial success as with artistic accomplishment. What he discovered, however, was a direction that would eventually lead him to the formation of a teachable system of acting.

3

Chekhov as Director and Teacher

Dartington Hall

While working in Germany, Chekhov's attention began to turn toward
establishing his own theatre, which would allow him to develop further his
ideas about the art of acting. Chekhov had become a successful actor in
Germany. In addition to the good public response to *Artisten*, he received
similar public acclaim for his comedic roles in German films. In spite of this
popularity with the German public, Chekhov was not satisfied with his work.
His notoriety was based primarily on comedic performances, not on serious
roles that he favored. In addition, he felt that he was in vogue as an actor
because of public fascination with a Russian emigré who had been a famous
actor in the Soviet Union. As a result, Chekhov began to formulate plans for
his own theatre that would appeal to a select group of people. He felt there was
an idea of a new theatre living in his soul.[1] This theatre would appeal to what
he described as an "ideal public," which was tired of the old, commercial
theatre; tired of theatre lacking great ideas, imagination and social meaning.
  Chekhov's ideas about his new theatre were nurtured by the visit of the
Habima Theatre to Berlin. Composed of Russian Jewish actors, the Habima
was founded by Alexander Granovsky in 1918.[2] Vakhtangov was influential
in the Habima's development and in 1922 directed its production of the
Dybbuk. Because of its admiration for Chekhov, the Habima asked him to
direct its new production of *Twelfth Night*, which it was adding to its
repertory. At this time, the Habima was touring Europe in order to make
enough money to establish a theatre in Palestine. Its hope was to show those
sympathetic to Zionism the importance of a theatre in Palestine. Chekhov was
inspired by the Habima's openness to new experiments in the theatre.[3] The
company was very close and worked diligently toward its goals with a tense
and active atmosphere. Such dedication to work Chekhov had not seen since
coming to Berlin. The Germans made fun of Chekhov for his long, strenuous
rehearsals for *Twelfth Night*. The Habima thrived on this type of rehearsal
process, but the Germans were used to working quickly. *Twelfth Night* was a

success throughout Europe and England. The Habima Theatre settled in Palestine in 1931 and is now the National Theatre of Israel.[4] This experience with the Habima strengthened Chekhov's resolve to form a new theatre; it confirmed his feelings that there were artists and a viewing public who would be interested in such an organization dedicated to new creative experiences. In preparation for this theatre, Chekhov began to attend a Rudolf Steiner school in Germany, working on eurhythmy and on Steiner's views of speech for the stage.

Chekhov thought he had the foundation for his theatre in Berlin where he began working with local Russian emigre actors. They worked on *Hamlet* with each actor playing several roles. Driven by a strong desire to establish the new theatre, Chekhov saw this *Hamlet* as a means to raise the necessary funds. After all, the German public was wild about Chekhov as the clown Skid. He thought that surely they would pay to see his work on Shakespeare's masterpiece. Unfortunately, Reinhardt was right. The German public did not want to see *Hamlet* at this time. They showed little interest in Chekhov's project, and it was a financial failure.

Chekhov was at a loss, not able to understand why he had failed, not knowing where to go or what to do next. He remembered the artists in Russia with whom he had worked so well and the Russian audiences for whom he had played Hamlet with great success. Then Georgette Boner, who was a student of Reinhardt's, invited Chekhov to come to Paris and start a theatre there. Chekhov had several friends in the large Russian emigre colony in Paris. Thinking that perhaps these fellow Russians would provide the artists and audience he needed, Chekhov left Berlin for Paris. When Chekhov arrived in Paris, however, he was again disillusioned. The Paris public wanted to see only the roles in which Chekhov was already successful. They were not as open to experimentation as he had hoped. Chekhov and Boner produced dramatizations of fairy tales based on Chekhov's idea that the wisdom of a race is found in its fairy tales.[5] This concept was to be developed more completely later at Dartington Hall, but the Paris audiences did not understand what Chekhov and Boner were trying to do.

Chekhov was again discouraged. However, the quixotic spirit in him led him to believe that there was an audience somewhere for his work. In 1933, two years after arriving in Paris, he left for Riga, where he directed Russian actors in the opera *Parsifal.*[6] He worked for a year in Latvia and Lithuania and established a theatre school in Riga in conjunction with the Latvian Actors' Union. This school later became an established theatre. Returning to Paris, Chekhov organized a company of Russian actors called The Moscow Art Players. These actors were former members of the Moscow Art Theatre, who were living in Paris and Germany at the time. Chekhov toured with this company to America and as a result of his exposure in the United States, he discovered an opportunity to start his new theatre.

The Moscow Art Players appeared in New York, Philadelphia and Boston during the 1934–35 season. In addition to Chekhov, the company included P. Pavlov, Vera Gretch, V. Solovieva, A. Bogdanov, G. Zagrebelsky, B. Alekine and B. Krementzky.[7] They performed in Russian seven plays in repertory: Gogol's *The Inspector General* and *Marriage,* Ostrovsky's *Poverty is No Crime,* Bulgakov's *White Guard,* Shkvarkin's *Strange Child,* Berger's *Deluge* and an evening of Anton Chekhov stories adapted for the stage by Mikhail Chekhov and P. Pavlov.[8] These productions, especially the "Chekhov Evening," were extremely successful. Brooks Atkinson called it "theatre liberated from the bonds of self-consciousness and imitations of life, and it is GLORIOUSLY REFRESHING on that account."[9] Gilbert Gabriel in the *New York American* stated: "I would join in granting them all the Moscow Art honors they deserve . . . hearty and lusty and mile-wide comical. I did not understand a single word of the Russian they were speaking. It is my pleasure to add that I DID NOT HAVE TO."[10]

Georgette Boner wired Beatrice Straight and Deirdre Hurst du Prey and told them that they must see Mikhail Chekhov. Boner knew that they were looking for a director for the theatre school at Dartington Hall in Devonshire, England. Mrs. Straight's mother and stepfather, Mr. and Mrs. Leonard Elmhurst, wanted someone to create a theatre program as part of their Department of Arts at Dartington Hall. Mrs. Straight and Mrs. du Prey had been touring the United States, searching for the right actor/director/teacher. When they saw Chekhov perform, first in *The Inspector General* and then in the Anton Chekhov one-acts, they were convinced that he was the person they needed. Mrs. Straight said she was impressed by him because his being was so full.[11] Deirdre Hurst du Prey said that watching Chekhov act was "like seeing a new planet. He had such qualities, such tremendous range in his acting. Colors were coming all the time; there was nothing hackneyed or usual. He was brilliant from beginning to end."[12]

Using Tamara Daykarhanova as a translator, these women talked with Chekhov at length about their plans. Dartington Hall was founded in 1925 as an experiment in rural development. It was built on the Dartington Estate as a center to meet the educational, social and cultural needs of the rural people in the area. Specifically, it was geared "to train boys and girls, and in addition, to supply teachers and workers who are competent to give direction and encouragement in the creative use of leisure."[13] At this time, departments of Agriculture, Horticulture, Forestry, Cidermaking and Textile Weaving were already established. There were also two schools, Elementary and Secondary, teaching male and female youths from the ages of two to eighteen. For the education and enjoyment of the adults of the area, there was a Department of Arts, including an Art Studio, Music Section, the Jooss-Leeder School of Dance, and the Ballet Jooss.[14] The Chekhov Theatre Studio was to be the final ingredient. Chekhov was very excited about their offer. He saw the possibility of directing a theatre, running a school and touring productions without any restrictions. The board of trustees of Dartington Hall accepted the recommendation to hire Chekhov and he spent the summer of 1935 at the home of Eugene Somov in Connecticut. He began to learn English and to organize his thoughts about the formation of his studio at Dartington Hall.

By September he knew English well enough to lecture in New York on the stages of the creative process. This lecture was attended by many members of the Group Theatre. Stella Adler and other members of this company were very impressed with Chekhov's performances and lecture and wanted to take classes from him. Harold Clurman stated:

> The actors [of the Group Theatre] felt that they had achieved some measure of honesty and truth in their work, but Chekhov's gift for combining these with sharply expressive and yet very free color, rhythm, and design was something in which they knew themselves to be deficient, and which they therefore envied. [15]

Other members of the Group Theatre, including Lee Strasberg, were not impressed with Chekhov and suggested that he be persuaded to return to the Soviet Union. [16] This argument was characteristic of the disagreements between factions led by Adler and Strasberg. Chekhov left for Dartington Hall in October and spent a year preparing for his new theatre. The Chekhov Theatre Studio opened on October 5, 1936.

Dartington Hall was the theatre for which Chekhov had been searching. There he was able to apply his ideas about theatre in an environment that was conducive to his work. There was no commercial pressure to succeed. Everything Chekhov wanted was provided by the Dartington trustees. His actors were young and enthusiastic. Essentially, Dartington was like a new version of the First Studio of the Moscow Art Theatre. It was a studio for experimentation and growth.

Chekhov approached the Studio with high ideals. He wanted "to make the Theatre representative of the best in contemporary thought and to use everything that was valuable in the drama of the past." [17] To this end he would explore the best of classical drama, but would also work with modern drama and plays for children. Chekhov felt that a key to understanding any culture existed in that culture's fairy tales, folk tales and fables. The experiments with fairy tales that he had begun with Georgette Boner in Paris were expanded at Dartington Hall. There was a fairy tale committee that researched and categorized fairy tales according to their subject matter. [18] For example, there were categories of wicked stepmothers, golden eggs, three brothers, etc. Chekhov's intention was to have a fairy tale company to play for children, which would benefit the actors as well as the children. He felt the world of the imagination was embedded in these tales and that by performing them, the actors' imaginations would be developed and set free. [19]

Chekhov stated nine aims for his Theatre Studio at Dartington Hall.[20] First, Chekhov sought to discover the essence of the playwright's intention in an effort to probe deeper into a play than most theatres were doing at the time. Mere imitation or a naturalistic representation of the play was not enough. In order to express the play's ideas, he felt one must probe beneath the surface, making the play and the work of the theatre expressive of important human issues.

To express these issues clearly, the second aim of the Studio was to closely examine and re-evaluate the tools at the actor's disposal. Chekhov felt that "all technique must be re-scrutinized and re-vitalized; external technique must be permeated by the power of a living spirit; inner technique must be developed until the capacity for receiving creative inspiration is acquired."[21]

Using a musical metaphor, Chekhov stated that the third aim of the Studio was to unify productions, composing them like a symphony. The fundamental laws of musical composition, harmony and rhythm were used to create a theatrical whole that would be understood by the audience, regardless of the language or intellectual content of the production. As a result, the production would affect the audience in the same manner as a musical composition.

In his fourth aim of the Studio, Chekhov expressed his uniqueness in mounting such productions. He advocated a new type of theatre artist capable of performing many artistic tasks. In spite of the genius of the specialized artists involved in mounting a production, Chekhov felt that to achieve the proper harmony, or unity of expression, the knowledge and experience of the specialized artist must be expanded. He observed that "an actor should, to some degree, be also a director, a scene painter, a costume designer, and even an author and musician; an author must know the psychology and practical needs of his actors; while a producer must be expert in lighting, decor and costume making."[22] Chekhov believed this new type of theatre artist would provide a collaborative production that was unified and more expressive of the human condition than most theatrical productions of the time.

The importance of theatre as an expression of the human condition led Chekhov to the fifth aim of his Studio. He felt that since the First World War, the emphasis on problems that affected people had shifted to include the sociological as well as the psychological and that it was the responsibility of his theatre to address these sociological problems. His theatre would provide a forum for studying the social problems affecting people at that time and possibly offer solutions. Individual human problems would be dealt with in relation to their social background.

Chekhov's next aim for the Studio further explains the way human problems would be explored. Chekhov saw his world going through a period of confusion and bewilderment and felt that as a result there was too much emphasis on what was morbid and unbalanced. To break away from this negative emphasis, his new Studio would "reveal the heroic in preference to the defeated and . . . recall the greatness of the human spirit in its age-long struggle with adversity."[23] As a result, the heroic quality of life would be explored and made a primary subject of this new theatre.

His seventh goal was to make humor a vital element in the Studio's productions. To Chekhov, humor was a way of lessening the world's difficulties. Chekhov next advocated a new type of play that would be the foundation of the new theatre. He felt that the theatre must eventually write its own plays, constructed to give his other aims for the theatre the greatest possibility of expression. Chekhov does not articulate what these new plays would be, but one assumes that they would encompass sociological problems, presented with an emphasis on the heroic qualities of life, and maximize the use of humor. At the same time, these new plays would have had to provide for many theatrical possibilities in order to nurture the talents of Chekhov's complete theatre artists. This was certainly no mean feat for the average playwright.

Finally, Chekhov aimed at exploring the relationship between his new theatre and its audience. He felt that if the theatre was to have meaning, the audience must be seen as a vital part. A close contact between the actor and audience was his goal. He advocated special periods when the theatre artists would work with a selected group of spectators to investigate the various problems that existed between the actor and audience.

These aims of Chekhov's Theatre Studio closely tied it to the First Studio of the Moscow Art Theatre. As stated earlier, Sulerzhitsky was interested in exploring the art of acting, making the actor more attuned to the playwright's work, and making the audience an integral part of the creative process. Chekhov's naive idealism was evident in his expansion of Sulerzhitsky's aims. These nine goals were admirable and intriguing, but virtually impossible to attain in any setting short of Utopia.

Chekhov developed a three-year training program for members of his Studio, after which members of the touring company would be selected. This program involved a detailed plan of study for training actors in his system of acting. Four categories of exercises made up the basis for this training program.[24] The first was geared toward the cultivation of concentration and the development of the imagination. The second was speech training, which followed the methods of speaking for the stage, developed by Rudolf Steiner.

In addition to following Steiner's views of Anthroposophy, Chekhov also had studied his method of speech formation in Germany. Steiner felt that speech was more than just an intellectual process of expressing ideas. To him, speech was a process of forming imaginative pictures through individual sounds.[25] Speaking was a process that began in the soul, and artistic speech, especially on stage, must express what was in the soul of the performer. Steiner felt this process must be taught because modern languages had lost their connection with the soul as a result of the limitations placed on them by modern conventions. These languages had become primarily a means of expressing the events of everyday life an did not express the psyche of those speaking. This artistic speech was possible only if one was aware of the connection between the soul and the sounds created in speech. For example, Steiner stated that a vowel sound was always expressive of some aspect of feeling: the sound "Ah" was expressive of wonder; "E" expressed self-assertion. Consonants, on the other hand, were expressive of things in the external world, things as perceived by the eyes.[26] According to Steiner, when one was aware of these concepts, speech became an artistic process and ceased to be simply an intellectual process.

Chekhov's students responded in various ways to this type of speech training. Beatrice Straight said that this method of training drew too much attention to the way an actor was speaking.[27] She said that it caused the actor to sing the lines of a role in a similar manner for every character that he/she was playing. Paul Rogers, now a successful British actor, had a different response to this speech training.[28] When Rogers began studying with Chekhov at Dartington Hall, he had a strong voice but it was not trained. The Steiner method of speech training helped him to improve the quality of his vocal rhythms and speech patterns. It helped make his speech expressive of his whole being.

The third type of exercise in Chekhov's training program was another concept developed by Rudolf Steiner. This was eurythmy, a movement art which made speech visible through the actor's physicalizations.[29] Eurythmy was an art of movement that differed from dance as an interpretation of music or speech, i.e., dancing to music or to the reading of a poem. With eurythmy, Steiner sought to actually make music or speech visible through the movements of the performer's body. It was the moving to speech, or making speech visible, on which Chekhov focused in his training. Concentrating primarily on the movements of the hands and arms, eurythmy taught the performer to be aware of three aspects of movement involved with the art: the nature of the movement itself, the feeling that lies within a particular movement and the character of a particular movement, which originates in the actor's soul.

Steiner's eurythmy is perhaps an extension of the eurhythmics of Emile Jaques-Dalcroze. Working as a music teacher in Switzerland, Dalcroze developed eurhythmics in 1897 as an educational tool for teaching music to children.[30] This concept developed into an art of kinesthetic awareness to the rhythms of music. The musician was taught how to respond physically and emotionally to rhythm. Dalcroze's work was later expanded to include the injecting of emotional values in movement for the stage and later had a strong impact on modern dance and actor training.[31] The difference between Dalcroze's eurhythmics and Steiner's eurythmy is that eurhythmics deals with the performer's kinesthetic response to rhythm, whereas eurythmy is an attempt to make music and/or speech visible to an audience through movement. Steiner states that eurythmy grew out of the Anthroposophical movement in 1912. To my knowledge, Steiner never relates it to Dalcroze's eurhythmics, developed almost twenty years earlier. However, Steiner seems to have taken the kinesthetic response of eurhythmics and expanded it into an art form of movement.

Paul Rogers claims that the eurythmy exercises of Chekhov's Studio were very helpful in "waking up" the actor's body, making it more expressive of the actor's creative impulses.[32] To complement this eurythmy approach, Chekhov had sculptors and painters come to the Studio and work with the actors. These artists had the actors work with clay and express themselves with chalk as they listened to music.

The fourth type of exercise in the Studio's training program dealt with the training and conditioning of the body. To this end, Chekhov provided training in fencing, acrobatics, tumbling and gymnastics. Chekhov stressed throughout his training program that the body should always be in perfect condition in order to withstand the physical demands of performance and to be able to perform any difficult physical action required by a particular role.[33]

Chekhov trained his students by working with them first on short scenes and improvisations.[34] As the students progressed, they were allowed to work on larger and more difficult pieces of dramatic literature. This work eventually led to the production of entire plays. As students worked on plays, they also studied musical compositions and were instructed in choral singing. This musical work, geared toward giving the actors a feeling for composition, harmony and rhythm, helped unify productions as it helped train the actors' voices.

Actors were also trained to design and build sets and costumes, to be proficient with makeup and to understand the uses of lighting.[35] With regard to lighting, Chekhov trained the actors to be sensitive to the effects of color on the emotions, as explained by Goethe's color theory.[36] Goethe was fascinated by the emotional and physiological effects color had on individuals. It is from Goethe's writings on this subject that Chekhov based his work with stage lighting. There was an experimental theatre at the Studio where students were required to practice what they learned about acting, directing, design and construction.

Actors in Chekhov's Studio performed scenes before selected audiences in order to explore the relationship between actors and audiences expressed in Chekhov's aims for the Studio. At the conclusion of the three-year course,

Chekhov planned to have the actors perform complete plays for a general audience as a culmination of the actors' training. Afterward, if they were selected, the actors were to prepare plays to be included in the repertory of the touring company. This touring group was important to Chekhov because it would provide secure employment for the actors and serve as a recruiting tool for the Studio.[37] Unfortunately, the full training program and the touring company were never realized because the Studio only lasted two years.

In spite of Chekhov's carefully laid plans and the apparent early success of the Chekhov Theatre Studio, events outside of Chekhov's control kept his aims from being fully realized. As the political events in Russia forced him to leave his homeland at the height of his acting career, so the coming of World War II to England forced the demise of his Theatre Studio at Dartington Hall. In the tragic and confused atmosphere of 1938, several male members of the Studio joined the British armed forces.[38] Meanwhile, the public did not want to see the type of theatre with a serious message that the Chekhov Theatre Studio was producing. Much like the German audiences that had disappointed Chekhov a few years earlier, the people of England wanted light entertainment to draw their attention away from society's problems. As a result, Chekhov's plan for a touring company was not feasible. The company had the opportunity to leave England, and they decided to do so while they still could.

Chekhov's plan was to go to America and start over with new people added to what was left of the Dartington company. Then after the war, the company would return to England and continue its work as originally planned.[39] This plan was never realized. After the war, some members had died in the fighting, and many other personal lives were changed so that a revival of the company in England was not possible. But in the two years of training at Dartington Hall, Chekhov had established a nucleus of students who were talented and dedicated to his work. Chekhov's Studio in America continued this work and spread his influence throughout the United States.

Ridgefield

When the decision to move the Studio was made, Beatrice Straight left for America to make necessary arrangements, while Deirdre Hurst du Prey stayed in England long enough to oversee the packing up of the Studio at Dartington Hall.[40] A good place for the new Studio was found, four miles from Ridgefield, Connecticut. The site included one hundred and fifty acres of land with enough buildings to supply large studios, a library, recreation rooms, dormitory rooms for students and a theatre.[41] This environment seemed to be ideal. It approximated the beautiful rural setting of the Dartington Hall Studio and was only fifty-five miles from New York City.

New students were auditioned for the Studio and the ones chosen joined the experienced students from Dartington Hall to begin the Ridgefield Studio in December of 1938.

In his statement of aims and purposes for the Ridgefield Studio, Chekhov simplified his original program. His nine somewhat lofty and vague aims for the Dartington Hall Studio were reduced to four more straightforward and practical ones for the Ridgefield Studio.

1. To apply a method of training which will develop emotional flexibility and body technique.
2. To develop a technique for the approach to the form and construction of plays.
3. To give the actor a practical opportunity to enrich his abilities through a knowledge of the methods and problems of the director.
4. At the end of this training period to form a professional company. [42]

There are three probable explanations for the tremendous differences between the statements of aims and purposes for the two Studios. It was not beneficial for the Studio to concern itself primarily with prevalent sociological issues. Even though America was not involved in the war in the winter of 1938, it was already becoming a concern for many Americans. Part of the problem that the Studio ran up against in England was that, because of their concern over the war, people were not attending theatre that probed serious social issues. They attended theatre that was entertaining and void of a serious message. The Ridgefield Studio would indeed produce theatre that dealt with the human condition, but it was not wise at the time to state that the Ridgefield Studio would become a forum for studying social problems.

Second, it appears that the aims stated for the Ridgefield Studio were geared to attract and appeal to American actors. These aims were made more systematic and tangible than those at Dartington Hall in an attempt to explain to prospective students what they would gain from studying there. A major difference between the Ridgefield Studio and Dartington Hall was that at Dartington Hall Chekhov had everything provided for him by the Dartington trustees. There was no economic pressure, no concern about paying the bills. This was not the case at Ridgefield. Although there were contributors, much of the money needed to keep the Studio running would come from student fees. As a result, it was imperative to attract students who were willing to pay the $1,200 per year fee for their involvement with the Studio. The actors paid for valuable training and the chance to be a part of Chekhov's professional company, which would provide additional training and some degree of financial security.

Third, the aims of the Ridgefield Studio were streamlined because Chekhov set to work at once on a production to guide the efforts of the Studio.

At Dartington Hall, the Studio had begun working on *The Possessed,* a series of improvisations and scenes based on Dostoyevsky's *Crime and Punishment, The Idiot* and *The Possessed.* Chekhov's idea was to continue this work at Ridgefield, preparing it for a Broadway production. Concerning this project's effect on the Studio's training, Chekhov stated, "We will eliminate certain things, and we will narrow the method down to these particular things that we require in our work. We shall stick to those related to our work in *The Possessed.*"[43] Hence, the thrust of the Ridgefield Studio immediately became more pragmatic. At Dartington Hall there was no pressure to produce a product. This situation fostered much experimentation and allowed Chekhov to pursue aims that were not easily defined. The economic realities in America changed that, and the work at Ridgefield was geared toward developing a successful Broadway show that would produce revenues to help sustain the work at the Studio.

Chekhov's description of the training program was also somewhat different for the Ridgefield Studio. The first two courses were titled simply "Technique of Acting" and "Training and Developing the Imagination,"[44] with no further descriptions. There was no mention of the development of the body through fencing, gymnastics, etc. The third and fourth courses were Steiner's Speech-Formation and Eurythmy with brief descriptions of each. The fifth was "Dramatic Studies, Improvisations and Scenes from Plays." The student would begin with short scenes and improvisations and then progress to more complicated dramatic problems. The student was also to receive basic instruction in design, lighting, makeup and the building of sets and costumes. Finally students had the opportunity to work as actors, producers, playwrights, scene painters and costume designers in an experimental theatre. The curricular items mentioned are virtually the same as those discussed in the course statement for the Dartington Hall Studio, but several items were omitted. There was no mention of the student's working on whole productions with emphasis on the thorough approach to the main idea of a play. There was no mention of the study of musical compositions and instruction in choral singing. There was no mention of lectures on theatre history and the writing of plays, and no mention of performing before a select group of spectators in order to explore the relationship between the actor and audience. The course items omitted were still an important part of actor training to Chekhov. He was still concerned with harmony and rhythm, the study of history, the relationship between actor and audience, etc. However, as a course of study, the Ridgefield curriculum differed in that it was pragmatic, included less experimentation and led to the performances of plays, the first of which was *The Possessed.*

In the spring of 1939, preparations were well underway for the coming production of *The Possessed.* The Studio formed a corporation called Chekhov Theatre Productions, Inc. to act as the producing group for its plays on Broadway.[45] At this time they intended to open *The Possessed* in the fall, followed closely by a production of *Adventures of Samuel Pickwick*, a play by Chekhov and Henry Lyon Young based on Charles Dickens's *The Pickwick Papers*. Once the corporation was formed, it set out to find a theatre for *The Possessed*. The results of the search were announced in the following press release:

> The Chekhov Theatre Productions, Inc., which is the professional producing outgrowth of the Chekhov Theatre Studio of Ridgefield, Connecticut, has signed contracts with the management of the Lyceum Theatre whereby that house will be the scene of its first Broadway production—a dramatization by George Shdanoff of Dostoievsky's novel, *The Possessed*, with ideas and themes embodied from other of his novels. Tuesday evening, October 24, has been set for the premiere.[46]

As an aid in helping the entire company prepare for *The Possessed*, Chekhov had his students in the advanced courses help teach the new students. Beatrice Straight, Deirdre Hurst du Prey and Blair Cutting were among those advanced students who had studied with Chekhov at Dartington Hall.[47] This method of teaching had two benefits. First, it helped the younger students learn the Chekhov system at a quick pace, and second, it taught the advanced students more about the system and their own creative work as they were teaching others. These three actors received certificates from Chekhov as teachers of his method and some members of this group are still teaching his method of acting today.

Unfortunately, the production of *The Possessed* was not as successful as the Studio had hoped. The production received mixed reviews and ran for only a month. Stark Young, writing for *The New Republic*, and Burns Mantle of the *New York Daily News* praised the ensemble of the company, their solid characterizations and their clear diction. However, other critics were not impressed. A vivid example of this negative reaction appeared in the *New York Times*. Brooks Atkinson wrote:

> Excepting one brilliant mob scene representing a revolutionary meeting, it comes close to being a travesty on the humorless manners of the Russian intelligentsia. Excepting that one scene, it conveys none of the spontaneity of a work of art ... [A] troupe of musclebound actors performs by rote. What a despotic dictatorship has done toward destroying the spirit of human beings in Russia, Mr. Chekhov has done to his actors here. Ironically enough, he has done it in a play that pleads the cause of the free man.[48]

However, even Atkinson's rather harsh comments were qualified. The one scene he mentioned, where a group of malcontents and intellectual fanatics met to attempt to reorganize humanity, he praised highly.

By applying his stylized method crisply, Mr. Chekhov has skillfully managed in this scene to satirize the cynical dogmatism of revolutionary leadership, the confusion of the party members and the excitement of people overwrought by diabolical forces that are sweeping them on. The scene has something to say, and says it without the dullness of a literal statement, meanwhile filling the theatre with sound, movement and frenzy. It has the genius of theatricalism.[49]

There were probably many reasons why the production of *The Possessed* was not received well on Broadway. Certainly, it was a difficult task for the Studio to mount such a production less than a year after it moved to America and added many new members to its company. Some members of the company felt that the trouble with the production resulted from not having a solid script from which to work. As stated earlier, the play was a series of fifteen scenes, which were basically recorded improvisations based on Dostoyevsky's novels. The script changed as the company rehearsed. This was disconcerting to some of the actors and the end product was confusing and too episodic.[50] Also, there may have been another factor in the negative critical response to *The Possessed*. Ford Rainey, a new member of the company at the time, was an extra in *The Possessed* and later acted in the Studio's touring productions as Sir Toby Belch in *Twelfth Night* and Lear in *King Lear*. Rainey's opinion was that the Studio set itself up to fail by the approach it took to publicity for the Ridgefield Studio and the production of *The Possessed*. Rainey stated:

The critics were ready to kill before each production of the Studio because the publicity was so bombastic. They were going to show America how it should be done. There was nothing subtle or humble in the publicity and people resented that. There was always this attitude of, "We are going to show you great acting."[51]

Because of the mixed success of *The Possessed,* Chekhov decided not to mount *Adventures of Samuel Pickwick* on Broadway and instead turned his attention to preparing a professional company to tour, fulfilling one of his major aims for his Studio. By the time the company began to tour in 1940, the students who were with Chekhov at Dartington Hall had worked with him for three years and the others had worked with him for over a year. This first tour included *Twelfth Night* and *The Cricket on the Hearth* and played to universities on the East Coast. It was a success from the beginning. As Chekhov planned, the tour provided professional work for the members of the Studio chosen to tour, it attracted additional students to the Studio and it was a testament to the success of Chekhov's acting system. Yul Brynner joined the Studio during this tour. His first job was driving the company truck on tour as he played Fabian in *Twelfth Night*. Brynner became enamored of Chekhov's system as evidenced by the preface he wrote for *To the Actor.*

The following year the tour was expanded. *King Lear* was added to the repertory and the company toured to the South and Midwest, as well as the East. The audience reaction to Chekhov's company was as positive in Mississippi and Oklahoma as it was on the East Coast.[52] Beatrice Straight and Blair Cutting were the artistic directors of the tour. They travelled with the company and ensured that the artistic integrity of the productions was maintained. As this professional company was showing much of the country the success of Chekhov's teaching and directing, he continued to teach and direct at the Studio in Ridgefield, periodically mounting productions at the theatre there.

In December of 1941, the company brought their production of *Twelfth Night* to Broadway for a limited engagement at the Little Theatre. The critical response was much better than it had been to *The Possessed*. Brooks Atkinson, who had attacked the Studio's first Broadway production, highly praised this one, with only slight criticism.

> Since the theatre sorely needs new ways to attack old problems, the Chekhov Players experiment is in the right direction. And when festive-minded Sir Toby and Maria have the stage, this version has both weight and gayety and it is wholly delightful.... *Twelfth Night,* how art thou translated! Call it the "Merry Adventures of Sir Toby Belch" and you can take a pleasant little holiday from the routine of hit-and-flop playgoing.[53]

The last appearance by the Chekhov Studio on the Broadway stage occurred in September of 1942, in a series of one-acts based on stories by Anton Chekhov. Two of these, *The Witch* and *I Forgot,* were performed by the Moscow Art Players when Mikhail Chekhov first appeared on the American stage. Chekhov again appeared in these plays, speaking in English this time, and the other plays were performed by members of his company. They included *Happy Ending* with Deirdre Hurst du Prey and David Heilweil, *After the Theatre* with Penelope Sack, and *The Story of Miss N. N.* performed by Beatrice Straight. The plays were performed at the Barbizon-Plaza as a benefit for the American-Russian Committee for Medical Aid to the Soviet Union. Chekhov's acting was praised very highly by several reviewers, but the reaction to his students was mixed. The reviewers' comments consistently commented on the students' performances being too labored and lacking spontancy.[54] These comments are also consistent with criticisms of *Twelfth Night* and *The Possessed*. Perhaps a reason for this was that the young actor-students of Chekhov were too conscious of their attempts to display what they had learned from him; they were trying too hard to perform well as Chekhov's students, instead of allowing the imagination and creativity which Chekhov had carefully developed to be expressed freely in their performances. Also, one must remember that most of these actors were still quite young and inexperienced. For the most part, they were not seasoned performers.

In spite of the mixed success of Chekhov's productions, his Studio at Ridgefield was successful. He had developed a good nucleus of students and his touring professional company was achieving the goals he envisioned. However, as at Dartington Hall, world events outside of Chekhov's control helped to put an end to an institution he had established. America's involvement in the war caused many of the male members of the Studio to be drafted into service, and the rationing of goods made it difficult to get the supplies needed to tour. Even tires for the company's station wagon were hard to obtain.[55] As a result, the Studio was forced to discontinue and once again, Chekhov had to find another outlet for his work.

His next move took him and his wife across the country to Hollywood. Gregory Ratoff persuaded Chekhov to move to Hollywood, where he could act in films and teach. Chekhov accepted the offer because the acting and teaching appealed to him and because he saw this as an opportunity to continue working on his book, the personal record of his acting system.

The evolution of this book into *To the Actor* was a complex one. Chekhov felt a personal obligation to record his views about acting, and so this project was very important to him. He began writing while working in Paris in the early 1930s. He and Georgette Boner worked on a German version of the book but it was never finished.[56] During the summer of 1935, while living in Connecticut before moving to Dartington Hall, he made notes for the book. Once the Dartington Hall Studio opened, he had Deirdre Hurst du Prey, his personal secretary, take notes on every class and every lecture at the Studio. He planned to use these extensive notes in writing the book. This careful record keeping continued after the Studio moved to Ridgefield. Paul Marshall Allen, an English professor interested in Rudolf Steiner, came to the Ridgefield Studio and expressed interest in helping Chekhov and Mrs. du Prey with the book. With Allen acting as editor, the book was completed in 1942. There were problems with this collaboration. Allen was apparently a good editor, but Chekhov felt that he over-edited the book, giving it correct English form and style but in the process losing the sense of what Chekhov was saying.[57]

When he went to Hollywood, Chekhov took this Allen-du Prey version of the book with him. However, he had difficulty finding a publisher, and he was not totally satisfied with the book's contents. Publishers were skeptical about the book's market value. With its many references to Anthroposophy and Steiner, they felt it was too spiritual and rarefied and not a down-to-earth "how to" book about acting. Chekhov's frustration over this response and his own dissatisfaction with its contents led him to rewrite the entire book in Russian and publish it himself. When *O texnike aktera (On the Technique of Acting)* was published in Hollywood at his own expense in 1946, Chekhov commented, "That was what I meant to say."[58]

Chekhov disseminated copies of *O texnike aktera* throughout the United

States, especially to those areas with a high concentration of Russian emigres. In addition, he sent copies to the Soviet Union with persons visiting there and with those returning after a visit to the United States.[59]

Chekhov then went through the difficult task of translating *O texnike aktera* into English, but he was not satisfied with the results. He came into contact with Charles Leonard, whom he asked to be editor for the book. Harper & Row became interested in the manuscript, and they began rewriting it for publication. The end result was *To the Actor on the Technique of Acting,* which was published in 1953. This is a useful book for actors and students of Chekhov's acting system. However, it does not include many of the allusions to Steiner and the intangibles of creative inspiration that are in the earlier versions. Deirdre Hurst du Prey is working at present on compiling all English versions of the book with her extensive notes of lectures and classes which were never used. It is hoped that her work will be concluded soon. It should prove to be a valuable asset to researchers and help provide an understanding of Chekhov's acting, teaching and directing techniques.

Hollywood

When Chekhov went to Hollywood in 1943, he acted in films, taught private lessons to film actors and gave lectures on acting and the creative process. He acted in nine films, playing character parts which were relatively easy for him. He told Ford Rainey that he did not particularly like the roles. At the beginning of one filming he said, "I'm playing another sweet little old man."[60] His first two films were released in the winter of 1944. *Song of Russia* was directed by Gregory Ratoff, who had persuaded Chekhov to come to Hollywood, and starred Robert Taylor. *In Our Time,* starring Ida Lupino, was released a month later in December of 1944. His next film gained him the most recognition. It was Alfred Hitchcock's *Spellbound* with Ingrid Bergman and Gregory Peck, a film for which Chekhov received an Academy Award nomination for best supporting actor. Concerning this performance, one reviewer wrote:

> Until Chekhov began operating in *Spellbound,* it was a soberly clinical picture. That does not mean it lacked fascination. It never does that, for it is always distinguished by the masterly technique of Director Alfred Hitchcock. Nor did it lack convincing playing, for Miss Bergman and Gregory Peck, as doctor and amnesia patient, respectively, can never be charged with ineffective performances. But it was coldly factual until Chekhov brought it the warmth of his personality and the charm of his characterization. He adds to it a lovable character in addition to giving it the benefit of yet another fine performance.[61]

Chekhov's other Hollywood film appearances included: *Specter of the Rose* (1946, with Dame Judith Anderson), *Cross My Heart* and *Abie's Irish Rose*

(1946), *Invitation* (1952, with Van Johnson and Dorothy McGuire), *Holiday for Sinners* (1952, with Gig Young and Keenan Wynn) and *Rhapsody* (1954, with Elizabeth Taylor). After Chekhov's second heart attack in 1954, he stopped acting and continued to lecture and teach acting.

Numerous film actors went to Chekhov for help with their specific roles and for their general acting development. They included in part: John Barrymore, Jr., Ingrid Bergman, Joan Caulfield, James Dean, John Dehner, Eddie Grove, Jennifer Jones, Jack Klugman, Sam Levine, Marilyn Monroe, Jack Palance, Gregory Peck, Mala Powers, and Anthony Quinn.[62] Three of these actors, Mala Powers, John Dehner and Marilyn Monroe, merit special discussion here because of their unique personal and professional relationships with Mikhail Chekhov.

Mala Powers, an accomplished screen actress, most widely known for her portrayal of Roxanne in José Ferrer's film of *Cyrano de Bergerac,* began working with Chekhov in the late 1940s. She took private lessons with him regularly and he helped her with every role she played until his death. She considered him to be an incomparable teacher.[63]

> One of the most outstanding characteristics about Chekhov, as a teacher, was that he viewed each artist as a unique creation; with an unknown, bottomless depth and capability slumbering within, which was constantly on the verge of awakening. Through working with Chekhov, one also came to feel this slumbering power within oneself—always ready to awaken. That was only one of the elements which made studying with Michael Chekhov so enormously exciting.[64]

After studying with Chekhov for six years, Mala Powers totally embraced Chekhov's system of acting. She credits his training with her success as an actress and his teaching is still the dominant influence in her professional life. However, Chekhov's influence went far beyond the many things he taught her about the art of acting. As they became close personal friends, he began to talk to her about his religious and philosophical beliefs. He never forced them on her but told her what he felt she needed and wanted to know. As a result, she also embraced his world outlook and became an Anthroposophist. She was very close to both Chekhov and his wife Ksenia, and when Ksenia died in 1971, Mala Powers became the executrix of the Chekhov estate.

Chekhov's effect on Mala Powers is indicative of the impact he had on almost everyone with whom he worked. This is not to say that many of his students became Anthroposophists. To many of his closest pupils, he never even mentioned Anthroposophy. However, almost to a person he touched the souls of those with whom he worked. Even if it was indirectly, he somehow taught them as much about themselves as he did about the art of acting. Mala Powers explained:

> The astonishing quality about him as a teacher was that nothing he ever taught related only to acting or to the theatre. Chekhov's method and manner of teaching was so completely based on deep truths that whatever one learned from him about art could also be applied to life, to a richer understanding and interaction with one's fellow man. He was concerned with the *whole* human being.[65]

John Dehner, who has had a very successful career as a film and television actor, was also very close to Chekhov.[66] Even though Dehner did not meet Chekhov until 1947, Chekhov had been an idol of his for many years. In 1935 Dehner went to New York to join a company called the New York Troupe, primarily because Chekhov was supposed to work with this company. As it turned out, Chekhov turned down this company's offer in order to go to Dartington Hall. Dehner finally met Chekhov in Hollywood and they became very close. Dehner regarded him as a surrogate father and was greatly influenced by Chekhov's system of acting.

From 1947 until Chekhov's death in 1955, Dehner organized many groups of actors for Chekhov to teach. Some of these actors had difficulty accepting Chekhov's methods. Dehner explained that the difficulty they had lay in the fact that they wanted everything put before them in practical terms. For example, Burt Lancaster got into a heated argument with Chekhov during one session when Chekhov explained that an actor must have total inner and outer freedom while performing. In this regard an actor should be like a trapeze artist who exhibits a free flowing form while performing at great heights. The actor should not be like a boxer who is grounded and violently struggles while performing. Lancaster said that Chekhov was crazy and that the boxer, who struggles with maximum physical effort, should be the actor's model.

Dehner stated that one of Chekhov's greatest attributes was that he was able to teach one how to be an "instant" actor, an actor who can fulfill all physical, emotional and psychological needs of the character instantly. There was nothing mystical about this process because Chekhov's exercises led one to this freedom of expression. It was very beneficial, especially to film actors, who had to create a moment quickly without the benefit of developing moments over a period of time as one does on stage.

The concept of psychological gesture was particularly helpful to Dehner. It was also particularly suited to films because it helped the actor to capture the essence of a character quickly. Once the psychological gesture was developed, it could be performed in rehearsal, or between takes to keep the character fresh and alive.

Even though his relationship with Chekhov was quite different, Dehner was as close, personally and professionally, to Chekhov as Mala Powers. However, Dehner was never drawn to Chekhov's Anthroposophy. Dehner said that Chekhov never mentioned Anthroposophy in classes and seldom mentioned it in their private talks.[67] Anthroposophy permeated Chekhov's system of acting but was a personal belief that was not part of his teaching. One's interest in or acceptance of this religious world view was not a prerequisite to acceptance of Chekhov's acting system.

It is interesting to note that even though Chekhov's system was developed for the stage, it became very useful for film actors. Chekhov was never pleased with the work being done in Hollywood during his time there. He felt that the work was too commercial and that the focus was more on mass entertainment than on genuine artistic creativity. However, he was pleased that any actor could use his system, and he was willing to help these film actors get the most out of their performance.

Perhaps Chekhov's most famous and, on the surface, most unlikely student during his years in Hollywood was Marilyn Monroe. Monroe began studying with Chekhov in the fall of 1951 at the suggestion of another successful actor enamored with Chekhov, Jack Palance.[68] Monroe was very interested in improving her acting talent and wanted parts that would challenge her ability. Chekhov was impressed with her acting potential from the beginning and encouraged her to develop her artistic gifts. As it turned out, Chekhov had a profound impact on her personal and professional life.

Not long before her death, Monroe gave a manuscript which she intended to develop into her autobiography to Milton Greene. Greene was a photographer and was responsible for forming Marilyn Monroe Productions, her own film company. In this uncompleted manuscript, which Greene published in 1974 under the title *My Story* by Marilyn Monroe, she devoted a section to Chekhov. The section is entitled "A Wise Man Opens My Eyes." In it she explained how Chekhov enabled her to see herself and her talent in a new light.

She had many acting lessons with Chekhov, whom she called "the most brilliant man I have known."[69] At times she jeopardized their relationship by not showing up for lessons or arriving very late. This problem grew worse until Chekhov suggested they stop meeting for a while. She apologized with a note saying, "Please don't give up on me yet—I know (painfully so) that I try your patience. I need the work and your friendship desperately. I shall call you soon."[70] Their lessons resumed on a regular basis.

One afternoon Monroe and Chekhov were working on a scene from *The Cherry Orchard* when he suddenly stopped and asked her if she were thinking of sex while they were playing the scene.[71] This took her completely by surprise, and she said that she was not thinking of sex, that her whole concentration was on the scene.

> He walked up and down a few minutes and said, "It's very strange. All through our playing of that scene I kept receiving sex vibrations from you. As if you were a woman in the grip of passion. I stopped because I thought you must be too sexually preoccupied to continue."
>
> I started to cry. He paid no attention to my tears but went on intently. "I understand your problem with your studio now, Marilyn, and I even understand your studio. You are a young woman who gives off sex vibrations—no matter what you are doing or thinking. The whole world has already responded to those vibrations. They come off the movie screens when you are on them. And your studio bosses are only interested in your sex vibrations. They care nothing about you as an actress. You can make them a fortune by merely vibrating in front of a camera. I see now why they refuse to regard you as an actress. You are more valuable to them as a sex stimulant. And all they want of you is to make money out of you by photographing your erotic vibrations. I can understand their reasons and plans."
>
> Michael Chekhov smiled at me.
>
> "You can make a fortune just standing still or moving in front of the cameras and doing almost no acting whatsoever," Michael said.
>
> "I don't want that," I said.
>
> "Why not?" he asked me gently.
>
> "Because I want to be an artist," I answered, "not an erotic freak. I don't want to be sold to the public as a celluloid aphrodisical. Look at me and start shaking. It was all right for the first few years. But now it's different."
>
> This talk started my fight with the studio.[72]

After this encounter with Chekhov, Monroe began a long period of struggle with 20th Century Fox over her desire to play more meaningful roles. The creation of Marilyn Monroe Productions with Milton Greene was one result of this struggle. Regarding her decision to reject the studio's million dollar offer if she would give up her ideas of being an artist, she said, "I wanted to be myself and not just a freak vibration that made fortunes for the studio sex peddlers."[73] Unfortunately, this conflict between herself and the studio, and between what the public came to expect of her and what she wanted to be, was never resolved. In the summer of 1962, the summer she died of a drug overdose, Monroe was immersed in a dispute with the Fox studio over the movie *Something's Got to Give*.[74] It is tragically ironic that Chekhov had such a positive influence on her life, but at the same time provided her with the personal revelations about herself and her career that in part contributed to her early death.

Chekhov was in poor health for most of his life, and the great difficulties of his career seemed to weigh heavily on his physical condition. With a history of heart trouble, he suffered a major heart attack during the filming of *Arch of Triumph* in 1948. The role he was to play in the film was taken over by Charles Laughton. After another attack in 1954, his career was virtually finished, although he continued to lecture and conduct private acting lessons until his death in 1955.

Mikhail Chekhov's fascinating life appears to have been filled with a series of false starts and frustrations as he sought to solidify his ideas about acting and create a new and vital theatre. Certainly he was victim to social and political turbulence, first in Russia, then in Europe, England and finally America. Twice it appeared that his ideal theatre was about to be realized when circumstances forced the theatre to be abandoned.

It is also possible, however, that the strength of his approach to theatre was also his undoing. This strength came from Chekhov's attempt to create the impossible. He sought to create an ideal actor who would collaborate with other total-artists, skilled in every aspect of theatre art, for the purpose of producing profound plays appealing to an ideal public. Such high idealism led Chekhov to significant discoveries about the art of acting, but it could never sustain a theatre organization. As his play *Don Quixote* indicates, Chekhov had a fondness for the idealist who tilted at windmills, regardless of the illogical and impractical nature of his actions. Chekhov was such an idealist. Although he failed to create a lasting theatre, his many efforts to do so were worthwhile, especially when seen as a background for the development of his acting theory.

Part Two

Mikhail Chekhov's System of Acting

4

Basic Requirements of Great Acting

If there is one aspect of acting that is the foundation of Chekhov's system, it is the actor's physicality. Both Deirdre Hurst du Prey and John Dehner claim that actor training for Chekhov begins with the physical.[1] Paul Rogers concurs that one of the most important things that he learned from Chekhov was that the actor must have a well-developed and expressive body capable of performing demanding tasks, and providing the actor endurance.[2]

According to Chekhov, the art of acting requires a special kind of physical development, and it is not sufficient to have simply a well-developed body. The body must be properly developed in conjunction with the actor's psychology. As a result, Chekhov espoused three requirements of great acting which unite the notions of physicality and psychology. Acting requires: (1) a sensitivity of the body to the psychological creative impulses, (2) a richness of the psychology itself, and (3) a complete obedience of both body and psychology to the actor.[3]

The term psychology can mean different things when applied to acting. When Chekhov uses the term, he refers to a trinity of thoughts, emotions and desires, each separate, yet dependent on the existence of the other two. Chekhov's first requisite of great acting, that the body must be sensitive to the psychology, stresses the importance of the psychology to any physical movement. Chekhov states, "The body of an actor must absorb psychological qualities, must be filled and permeated with them so that they will convert it gradually into a sensitive membrane, a kind of receiver and conveyor of the subtlest images, feelings, emotions and will impulses."[4] Chekhov deplores what he refers to as a materialistic world outlook, which has been dominant since the latter part of the nineteenth century. This view of life and art which emphasizes realism has caused people to be mechanical and ordinary in their physical expression, and has caused a gulf between a person's body and what that person thinks, feels and wants. On stage, the result is clichéd movement that is devoid of creative expression.

This fascination for reality has also caused actors to neglect the difference between everyday life and life on the stage. Chekhov feels that actors who attempt to reproduce real life on stage exactly as they observe it become photographers and not artists of the stage. They see their job as copying the outer appearance of life, instead of interpreting life, showing what is behind the phenomena of everyday life. To counteract the negative influences of materialism, the actor must work in a systematic way to explore the imagination and focus on those impulses which are antithetical to a materialistic way of living and thinking. The actor's body should be re-created from the inside and developed so that it is motivated by artistically creative thoughts, emotions and will. The first nine exercises in *To the Actor* are designed to help the actor's body be more expressive of the psychology.

Chekhov's second requirement of great acting, enriching the psychology itself, is one of the most intriguing and attractive aspects of his acting system. This concept is not unique to Chekhov's system, but his manner of articulating it is novel and reveals much about Chekhov himself. Chekhov talks about the importance of penetrating the psychology of persons from different historical periods, realizing that human psychology is constantly changing. In the same vein, one should also attempt to penetrate the psychology of persons from different countries, focusing on the differences between people of different nations.

The most intriguing aspect of developing the psychology itself, however, is the penetration of the psychologies of those persons toward whom the actor feels unsympathetic. Your own psychology is enriched tremendously if you can understand the feelings and actions of those persons you do not like, if you can put yourself in their shoes. Chekhov says:

> Remain objective and you will enlarge your own psychology immensely. All such vicarious experiences will, by their own weight, sink gradually into your body and make it more sensitive, noble and flexible. And your ability to penetrate the inner life of the characters you are studying professionally will become sharper. You will first begin to discover that inexhaustible fund of originality, inventiveness and ingenuity you are capable of displaying as an actor. You will be able to detect in your characters those fine but fugitive features which nobody but you, the actor, can see and, as a consequence, reveal to your audience.[5]

It is not unique to talk about the importance of actors understanding and getting along with persons they do not like, especially as it relates to developing characters unlike one's self and establishing a productive working atmosphere among a group of diverse artists. However, I know of no other actor or theorist who articulates this concept as clearly as Chekhov or who makes it an integral part of an acting system. It is a cliché that we should all love each other. But no one has delved so deeply into the importance of love for the actor as Mikhail Chekhov.

In his lecture "Love in Our Profession," Chekhov develops this concept more completely, and it has direct bearing on his notion that an actor's psychology must be enriched.[6] In this lecture, Chekhov says that love is a treasure within our souls, having great creative potential. When he uses the word "love" in this context he means the highest form of love between human beings. It is a love of every human being without any restrictions of sex, blood relationships, or ego. This human love is a positive power working within us, and actors must be aware of it and allow it to grow. As Chekhov articulates it, the knowledge and development of human love has practical applications to the art of acting.

A practical result of this knowledge and development of human love comes from the fact that all creative feelings are based on this love, and are generated by it. In talking about creative feelings, Chekhov makes a clear distinction between the creative feelings an actor experiences on stage and the real feelings in everyday life. This concept will be developed more completely later when I discuss Chekhov's ideas about an actor's individual feelings. For now it is enough to know that Chekhov's distinction between these two types of emotions is grounded on the idea that on stage all creative feelings are based on love. For example, if a character hates someone or something on stage, the actor in a sense enjoys this hating because it is based on love. He/She is not actually hating as he/she does in real life. Chekhov contends that if one does not base the creative feelings on stage on human love, one brings real feelings from everyday life to the stage and, as a result, kills art. Developing the knowledge and potential of human love preserves art and allows one to grow and develop as an artist and as a human being.

Another application of this concept of human love for the artist derives from the fact that human love's strongest characteristic is expansion. This love is not static but is constantly moving. As it develops, one's talent expands and one develops as an artist. The negative forces within us cause our talent to contract and our creative being to diminish. But by nurturing our human love, we constantly expand our talent and creativity.

The third way in which this human love applies to the art of acting is that the essence of the acting profession is giving. Chekhov claims that as actors we give our body, voice, feelings, imagination, will, everything to our characters. We also give everything to the spectator. Giving, the most characteristic feature of acting, and expansion,, the most characteristic feature of human love, are identical as they relate to an audience. Love expands the actor's individual talents but it also draws the actor and audience together. If an actor uses this concept, the character will be a creation of one's creative self and will reach out to the audience. The actor who is not aware of the possibilities of human love is an egoist on stage and cuts himself off from a full audience communication. An added benefit of this technique is that it gives the actor confidence and peace of mind, which come from expanding and giving.

In his taped lectures, Chekhov gives suggestions for the development of human love in the artist. One of these suggestions applies directly to the statement in *To the Actor* concerning the development of the psychology. He says:

> As soon as you see something ugly around you, try to see at least a grain of something which is not ugly, not repulsive. In everything which is unpleasant it is possible to find something which is pleasant. This will send a signal to the essence of your human soul which will help to awaken what we call love.[7]

As intangible as this concept of love seems, if an actor makes conscientious use of it, its usefulness will be evident. As with many of Chekhov's statements about acting, this concept of human love takes an abstract idea and develops it into a workable technique for the actor. Chekhov is striving for the development of artists who are interested in exploring creative acting to the fullest. He has no use for the limitations of pragmatism or materialism. By exploring the creative process with as much love and freedom as possible, he aims at training actors who can interpret life in their own way. As a result, the love of all human beings becomes a skill that the actor develops and then uses to create roles and to share these roles with audiences.

Chekhov again touches on this second requirement of acting, the enriching of the psychology, in his lecture entitled "Ensemble Feeling." While talking about developing this feeling with one's partners on stage, Chekhov says that even though we will always like one person more than another, on stage we must find the inner power to be friendly toward everyone regardless of our personal attitude.[8] If you do not enjoy being with a fellow actor, you should try to enjoy his acting. Otherwise, you will always seem isolated on stage. If you enjoy his acting, you are to some degree brought together with this person even if the person does not return it. If you do not enjoy his acting, find some small quality about him or his performance that you do like. This little thing will grow as you work and you will find more and more to like about him, which will strengthen the ensemble feeling between you.

Then Chekhov takes up a favorite topic, criticism. He says, "Indifference is bad enough. Criticism is a crime."[9] Avoiding criticism of one's self and of others is a recurring idea in Chekhov's scheme of things. Criticism is one of those negative forces within us that Chekhov was convinced would contract our talents if we let it develop. He suggests that one should be aware of these negative forces but allow the positive ones, like human love, to develop and rule. Furthermore, "if, in addition to the foregoing suggestions, you acquire the habit of suppressing all unnecessary criticism, whether in life or in your professional work, you will hasten your development considerably."[10]

Chekhov's third requirement of great acting is the complete obedience of both body and psychology to the actor. Regardless of how sensitive the body is to the psychology, or how well the psychology is developed, they are worthless unless the actor has the ability to use them at will. Chekhov emphasizes this point by saying:

> The actor who would become master of himself and his craft will banish the element of "accident" from his profession and create a firm ground for his talent. Only an indisputable command of his body and psychology will give him the necessary self-confidence, freedom and harmony for his creative activity.[11]

This third requisite is the most straightforward of the three, but it is probably the most important because Chekhov's entire system of acting leads to the accomplishment of this requirement. In other words, his system is above all one that leads the actor to have complete control over his/her instrument. It is important to keep this point in mind because often the abstruse nature of Chekhov's creative ideas leads people to consider his system esoteric or mystical. However, when one works with Chekhov's system, it can become very clear and very useful. He conscientiously probed the depths of the creative process and delved into philosophy and religion. But there is nothing esoteric about his acting system. It is accessible without being merely pragmatic. It is an acting system that takes intangible concepts and makes them useful, creative tools of the actor.

The first several exercises in the first chapter of *To the Actor* are aimed at providing freedom and ease of movement and at strengthening the bond between the body and psychology. They have actors exploring expanding and contracting movements, moving from an imaginary center in the chest, molding the space around them as they move, exploring floating and flying through space, and using radiation. What connects these physical movements to the psychology is the concentration on specific psychological states that go along with the exercises. For example, while performing the expanding movements of the first exercise, the actor says to himself, "I am going to awaken the sleeping muscles of my body; I am going to revivify and use them."[12] While doing the floating movements of the fourth exercise, the actor says to himself, "My movements are *floating* in space, merging gently and beautifully one into another."[13] These statements give the physical movements a purpose and direction, while they help make the actor aware of the effect these movements have on the psychology.

Eddie Grove, an actor who studied with Chekhov in Los Angeles in the early 1950s, now teaches Chekhov's acting system in New York City. He uses these exercises every class period as a warm-up. Commenting on their usefulness, Grove says, "One cannot make a gesture without experiencing something, but most actors today are too divorced from their psychology. The body must be converted to a sensitive membrane that can radiate things to spectators. If Chekhov's exercises are practiced regularly, that result will be achieved."[14]

It is important to Chekhov's system that actors involve themselves totally in each exercise and that each exercise be performed with the purpose of developing the actor into an artist. After having the actor work through the molding movements, Chekhov says:

> Having acquired sufficient technique in doing these molding movements, and experienced pleasure in making them, next say to yourself: "Every movement I make is a little piece of art, I am doing it like an artist. My body is a fine instrument for producing molding movements and for creating forms. Through my body I am able to convey to the spectator my inner power and strength." Let these thoughts sink deeply into your body.[15]

This molding exercise gives the actor a taste for form and, like many of the other exercises, gives the actor an awareness of movements that are free, expressive and artistically created.

Perhaps the two most interesting and unique exercises of Chekhov's acting system are the ones dealing with moving from an imaginary center and using radiation. These exercises are tremendously helpful in developing presence and self-confidence on stage. With these exercises, you imagine an imaginary center within your chest from which flows the actual impulses for all movements. This center is a source of power which begins within the chest and flows throughout the body. You imagine that your arms and legs actually originate from this center within the chest. As you move, the power that flows from the imaginary center precedes the movement and follows after the movement is made. In other words, while performing a movement, you send out or radiate the impulse for the movement ahead of you, physically perform the movement and then let the power of the movement radiate beyond the boundaries of your body, filling the space in which you are working.

Many acting teachers and theorists use the concept of centering but Chekhov's notion differs in that it is always linked to radiation. Chekhov contends that as long as the imaginary center is in the chest, the actor's body approaches an "ideal" that allows the actor to make the greatest possible use of his body. This "ideal" body can be compared to a well-tuned musical instrument. I will discuss how centering is applied to the physicality of a character when I talk about Chekhov's approach to characterization. Basically, the actor places the imaginary center in the part of the body that best expresses the center of the character. The center may also be placed outside of the body, as Richard Kiley did in *Man of La Mancha*. Kiley placed Don Quixote's radiating center just above his forehead and in front of his body.[16]

Radiation of the center allows a character to be communicated to the audience in a powerful manner. It gives an actor presence and the character enough power to communicate to the entire audience. In Eddie Grove's acting classes, he requires the actors to work to establish the radiation throughout their bodies, and then perform natural gestures and movements with this radiation.[17] Grove uses radiation as a warm-up exercise in his classes, but he also teaches actors to use radiation in performance, in order to strengthen the contact between themselves and the audience. Chekhov articulates another benefit of radiation by saying:

> A sensation of the actual existence and significance of your *inner being* will be the result of this exercise. Not infrequently actors are unaware of or overlook this treasure within themselves, and while acting rely far more than necessary upon merely their outer means of expression. The use of outer expressions alone is glaring evidence of how some actors forget or ignore that the characters they portray have living souls, and that these souls can be made manifest and convincing through powerful *radiation*. In fact, there is nothing within the sphere of our psychology which cannot thus be radiated.[18]

Chekhov contends that an actor's physical movements on stage must involve four qualities of movement: Ease, Form, Beauty, and Entirety. He says that these qualities are present in every great work of art.

Beginning with the quality of ease, Chekhov says that heaviness is an uncreative and destructive power that can depress and repulse an audience. A character may be heavy, awkward and inarticulate, but the actor must use lightness and ease as a means of expression. It is extremely important to distinguish between what actors perform and how they perform it. The how always involves a feeling of ease, regardless of the presence of a heavy character or theme. Chekhov also relates this ease to humor. The comedian who is most successful performs all of his/her actions with ease. Chekhov points out that the exercises dealing with flying and radiating movements are particularly helpful in acquiring this quality of ease. Beatrice Straight uses the quality of ease more than any other Chekhov technique except psychological gesture. She says it helps her to envelop the audience in a live performance.[19]

Understanding the difference between the what and how of a character is also crucial to the development of the quality of form. Regardless of how chaotic or formless the character may be (the what), the actor must perform this character with a perfect and complete feeling of form (the how). The exercises on the molding movements are helpful in developing this feeling of form. As Chekhov says in this section:

> You will develop a taste for form and will be artistically dissatisfied with any movements that are vague and shapeless, or with amorphous gestures, speech, thoughts, feelings and will impulses when you encounter them in yourself and others during your professional work. You will understand and be convinced that vagueness and shapelessness have no place in art.[20]

The development and use of the quality of beauty for the actor is also a matter of distinguishing between the what and how of a character. But Chekhov first points out that one needs to realize that there is a positive and negative side of beauty. He states, "True beauty has roots *inside* the human being, whereas false beauty is only on the outside. 'Showing off' is the negative side of beauty, and so are sentimentality, sweetness, self-love and other such vanities."[21] So the actor must focus on this inner beauty and not a surface beauty that leads to egotism. With that in mind, one approaches beauty through the what and how of the character as with the other qualities. Ugliness or an unpleasant theme, character or situation played with the quality of beauty makes this unpleasantness appealing to the audience. Without beauty as the how of expressing this unpleasantness, the audience will be irritated and react physiologically to the unpleasantness, instead of reacting psychologically to an artistic creation.

The quality of beauty seems to relate to Chekhov's concept of human love discussed earlier. All creative feelings are based on human love, which seems to be the same thing as the inner beauty Chekhov refers to here. When a character hates on stage, the audience is attracted to this hating because the emotion is based on love, just as the audience is attracted to unpleasantness on stage because the unpleasantness is performed with the quality of beauty.

Chekhov's concept of beauty was partly influenced by the work of Alexander Tairov at the Kamerny Theatre. In one of his lectures on the great Russian directors, Chekhov states:

> Behind all his [Tairov's] flossy and glossy creations there was an arresting quality that defies definition. It was extreme beauty, to be sure, but also had strong, undeniable undercurrents of earnestness and sincerity. It was more than beauty for the eye alone. He expressed himself and the meaningful things of his plays through the *soul* of beauty.[22]

The quality of entirety requires the actor to perform with a sense of the whole, not in separate and unrelated moments. Without the quality of entirety, the performance will be inharmonious and incomprehensible to the audience. Chekhov explains that:

> ...if in the beginning or from the very first entrance you already have a vision of yourself playing (or rehearsing) your last scenes—and, conversely, remembering the first scenes as you play (or rehearse) the very last scenes—you will better be able to see your whole part in every detail, as though you were viewing it in perspective from some elevation.[23]

Performing with the quality of entirety will enable the actor to blend details harmoniously. In addition, the actor will play the essentials of the character and still follow the main line of events, producing a powerful character that is well integrated.

Chekhov's acting system offers an approach to acting that is contemporary. Its emphasis on developing and expressing the actor's physicality is compatible with the emphasis upon physical training that is used by many actor training programs today. Much of this emphasis on developing the full potential of the body is an outgrowth of the alternative theatre experiments of the 1960s, which heightened people's awareness of the body's power of expression and the importance of its development in training actors.

In a recent article in *The New York Times Magazine* on contemporary actor training, Richard Schechner, acting chairman of New York University's performance studies department, comments on the importance of training the body by saying, "The body thinks now. It's entitled to, and I think the experimental theatre of the 1960s had something to do with that. We're much more into physicalized theatre."[24] The thrust of this article is that, as a result of physicalized training and emphasis on technique, contemporary actors are more versatile than American actors were twenty years ago. Actors such as William Hurt, Meryl Streep and Kevin Kline, who were trained in acting conservatories, are able to perform equally well in classic, realistic and absurdist dramas on stage and in films.[25]

Chekhov's acting system fits well into this new approach because it begins with the actor's physical resources and then proceeds to techniques which are keys to unlocking the actor's creative expression. It is a system that leads the actor to inspired acting in a manner appropriate for any type of role.

5

Keys to Expression

Imagination, Improvisation, and Ensemble

Now that we have seen how Chekhov's approach to the actor's body and psychology form the ground work for his acting system, it is important to examine the means for unlocking the actor's creative expression. This process begins with the actor's imagination, one of the most important elements of Chekhov's system. For him the imagination is a powerful force that takes everyday people and events and transforms them into creative images. These creative images have a life of their own and are constantly changing; they are full of emotions and desires. But in order for them to be useful for the actor, they must be nurtured and developed.

In the second part of his lecture on characterization, Chekhov says that the imagination must be developed through constant practice. In order for actors to transform themselves into their characters, actors must be able to open themselves to people who are objects of observation, and then use their imaginations to transform themselves into these people being observed. This observation should be a daily practice for actors, because the more they use the imagination to transform themselves into people being observed, the better able they are to transform themselves into a character for the stage. [1]

Also in this lecture, Chekhov gives exercises for the developing of the imagination. He suggests that the actor observe the face of a person whom the actor does not know. This actor then uses the imagination to feel that the other person's features are on his own face. For example, the actor imagines that he has the nose, eyebrows, forehead, etc., of the other person. As the actor is doing this, he is also trying to penetrate the psychology of the observed person. This is an important point because it ties into Chekhov's other exercises devoted to developing the psychology. As I stated before, almost all of Chekhov's exercises involve the actor's entire being. Everything the actor has to work with—the body, voice, psychology, imagination, etc.—is integrated in such a way that concentration on one part will have an effect on the other part. Chekhov does not speak about individual tools of the actor. He speaks about the actor's entire being, which is integrated in such a way that an exercise for the imagination will automatically affect the psychology, and vice versa.

Developing creative images from real-life people and events requires the active collaboration of the actor, because these images often will not appear on their own. To make use of these images, Chekhov says, "You must ask questions of these images, as you would ask questions of a friend. Sometimes you must even give them strict orders. Changing and completing themselves under the influence of your questions and orders, they give you answers visible to your inner sight."[2]

Chekhov cautions against overusing analytical reasoning in deciding how a character should be played. Imagination provides a much more creative way of discovering who a character is and how the character reacts to other characters and the situations of the play. The actor uses this imagination early in the rehearsal process by asking his/her character how he/she would act in each scene of the play. For example, if you were playing Malvolio in *Twelfth Night* and working on the scene where he approaches Olivia in the garden, you might ask your image of Malvolio, "Show me, Malvolio: how would you enter the gates of the garden and with a smile move toward your 'sweet lady?'"[3] Once the question is asked, your image of Malvolio will begin to act for you. Through your creative imagination, you will see the character reacting to the situation and the questions you ask of it. But more specific questions are often necessary. You may have to ask it to show you specific details of the character's expression and/or movement. If you are dissatisfied with what you see in your imagination, you may have to ask it more questions or order it to show you different approaches the character might take.

As you are involved in this process, you are actively collaborating with your creative imagination. Chekhov cautions that answers do not always come quickly. Often you may be dissatisfied with what you first see in your imagination. However, if you continue to work at it, continue to ask your image of the character questions and give it orders, you will eventually find the answers to the questions of how the character should be played. Also, as I said before, this work with the imagination will affect your entire psychology and you will have a strong desire to act. Such results cannot be achieved through reasoning alone. Chekhov says:

> By working this way you will be able to study and create your character more profoundly (and more quickly, too); you will not be relying only on ordinary thinking instead of "seeing" these little "performances." Dry reasoning kills your imagination. The more you probe with your analytical mind, the more silent become your feelings, the weaker your will and the poorer your chances for inspiration.[4]

Chekhov contends that this work with the creative imagination is just as successful, and perhaps even more necessary, when one is working on modern plays with characters similar to those people we see in everyday life. Actors are mistaken when they assume that since a character is similar to themselves, all they have to do is perform the playwright's actions and lines in order to bring the character to life. Such an attitude robs actors of their creative contribution to the play and produces characters who are shallow and uninteresting. According to Chekhov, the actor's job should be to discover and express the psychological depths of the character. Since no human being is easy to understand, the discovery of the character's psychological depths requires much work and probing by the imagination. Chekhov feels that one of the major problems with modern actors is that too many of them present themselves on stage and endow their characters with their own personality and mannerisms. An actor should never present himself directly on stage, but should develop a character mask, which is a product of the actor's imagination. Chekhov says that without such a mask, the actor leaves the frame of art and can play only "straight" parts.[5] This problem will be discussed in more detail later when I talk about Chekhov's approach to characterization. If an actor is to get beyond his own personality and have the freedom to create new and original characters, he must make use of the creative imagination. Chekhov says that "the creative imagination is one of the main channels through which the artist in him finds the way to express his *own,* individual (and therefore always unique) interpretation of the characters to be portrayed."[6]

Chekhov suggests that it is more beneficial for the actor to work on one aspect of the character at a time to avoid the difficulty of incorporating the entire image at once. Working gradually on building the overall image from smaller ones will allow one to incorporate all aspects of the character into a unified whole. An additional benefit of this image work is that it helps in the development of the actor's body. Incorporating strong images helps mold the body from within, making it more sensitive to the psychology in the manner previously discussed.

In laying the groundwork for his ideas on improvisation, Chekhov says in *To the Actor* that all artists have the desire to express themselves freely and completely. Those who succeed do so by improvising with the tools of their particular art form. The actor is no different from other artists in this respect, and he can express himself freely and completely only through free improvisation. An actor who is limited merely to speaking the lines of the role and performing the actions indicated by the playwright and director is not a creative artist. The actor should instead take advantage of the opportunity to improvise that exists in every role. Chekhov is not talking about inventing new lines or different movements than the director has indicated. These lines and bits of business are the framework upon which the actor builds his improvisations. The "how" of the role is what is left up to the actor to create. *"How* he speaks the lines and *how* he fulfills the business are the open gates to a vast field of improvisation. The 'hows' of his lines and business are the ways in which he can express himself freely."[7]

In addition, the many moments between the lines and indicated actions are open to the actor to improvise freely and creatively. Such improvised moments will help the actor approach the entire part as his own interpretation, a new creation that is different from the actor's own personality and void of clichés. Improvisation is one method of developing this new creation. It is a skill that needs to be recognized and developed.

Chekhov used this skill masterfully in his own performances. Vasili Toporkov, the Russian actor, director and teacher of Stanislavsky's method, was greatly impressed with Chekhov's use of improvisation. His comments provide a vivid example of Chekhov's concept of improvisation.

> His [Chekhov's] extraordinary improvisations occurred during actual play productions. Every performance was a new creation. Theatre buffs in Moscow would go time after time to see the famous lying scene in Gogol's *Inspector General;* each time they saw it Michael Chekhov would amaze them with his unexpected improvisations, with the subtle nuances he gave to the typical traits of Gogol's hero. The very way in which Chekhov improvised coincided with the character of Khlestakov—an improviser of fantastic lies in the mayor's house. But I must point out that while he interpreted the part in that way, Chekhov never violated Gogol's text, never added or cut a single line. His improvisations were truly brilliant models, illuminating Gogol's literary masterpieces in terms of theatre.[8]

Chekhov's exercise for improvisation is a very useful one. He suggests that the actor decide on the beginning and ending moments of the improvisation and define only the mood or feelings of the beginning and end. The entire transition from beginning to end is what the actor improvises. This transition is a series of successive moments that develop psychologically as the actor works. By focusing on the psychological development from moment to moment, and not a logical progression, the entire gamut of thoughts, feelings and will impulses will be opened up and the intellectual process will be de-emphasized. Once this improvisation is completed, it should be repeated, leaving one's self open to new discoveries, repeating exactly only the beginning and ending moments. Next, one should add another point in the middle of the improvisation, another definite action with a defined mood or feeling, and then improvise from beginning to middle to end. Once this process has been explored, more points are added at random so that the structure becomes more complex. Eventually, one has an improvisation that resembles the structure of a scene from a play. However, to keep the improvisation from becoming static, the structure should be changed, perhaps even transposing the beginning and end. Also, different atmospheres, changing tempos or other given circumstances added to the improvisation will preserve the improvising spirit of this exercise.

There are many benefits to be derived from this exercise. I have found it to be a great help to actors who have a tendency to speak their lines mechanically and perform their blocking in a lifeless manner. It can also add life and creativity to an actor who may be technically proficient but dull and lifeless on stage. In articulating the benefits he sees from the exercise, Chekhov says:

> The result of this exercise is that you develop the *psychology of an improvising actor.* You will retain this psychology while going over all the necessities you have chosen for your improvisation, regardless of their number. Later on, when rehearsing and performing on the stage, you will feel that the lines you have to speak, the business you have to do and all the circumstances imposed upon you by the writer and director, and even the plot of the play, will lead and direct you as did the necessities you found for your exercise. You will not notice any substantial difference between the exercise and your professional work. Thus you will eventually be confirmed in the belief that dramatic art is nothing more than a *constant improvisation,* and that there are no moments on the stage when an actor can be deprived of his right to improvise. You will be able to fulfill faithfully all the necessities imposed upon you and at the same time preserve your *spirit of an improvising actor.* A new and gratifying sensation of complete confidence in yourself, along with the sensation of freedom and inner richness, will be the reward of all your efforts.[9]

These improvisation exercises are as valuable for groups of actors as they are for the individual. These exercises can and should be used with groups of two or more in much the same way, except that the focus shifts from the individual to the development of the ensemble. Chekhov contends that regardless of how talented an individual actor may be, he will not be able to develop fully the ability to improvise if he is isolated from his fellow actors. A sensitivity to the creative impulses of others is required. As a result, exercises dealing with group improvisation and consequently successful performances on stage depend on the development of what Chekhov calls ensemble feeling. In Chekhov's lecture entitled "Ensemble Feeling," he describes this concept in more detail and expands the notion discussed in *To the Actor.*[10]

In this lecture, he begins by saying that there are many inhibitions that hinder an actor's work, and if they are not rooted out, they prevent the actor from progressing. A lack of ensemble feeling is one of the greatest inhibitions. One aspect of this ensemble feeling is an openness with the other actors with whom one works. This is the process of giving and taking Chekhov discusses in *To the Actor.* Once this ensemble is established, he says, "A small hint from a partner—a glance, a pause, a new or unexpected intonation, a movement, a sigh, or even a barely perceptible change of tempo—can become a creative impulse, an invitation to the other to improvise."[11]

However, in a broader sense, ensemble feeling is more than establishing contact with the people around us. As Chekhov articulates in his lecture, it should also exist in our contact with the setting, properties and costumes—everything that affects our characters on stage. As actors, we are never totally comfortable on stage without an ensemble feeling with the setting. In order to achieve this, Chekhov suggests that we begin in rehearsals being aware of everything around us. We should try to absorb these things, not just look at them. This applies to every part of the setting, even those parts our characters never use. As much as possible, the setting should become our home; we should believe that the setting consists of our room, our chairs, etc. Establishing this ensemble feeling with the setting allows us to play within it with freedom and pleasure.

This same ensemble feeling should be established with the properties and costumes. Properties often disturb actors. Chekhov says that if they are not friendly they are enemies and, as a result, cause inhibitions. We must absorb the properties, as we do the setting, making them ours, If we do, they stop being inhibitions and become helpful in developing and expressing our characters. Chekhov says of costumes, "often we put them on and feel as if we are in a coffin."[12] When this happens, the costumes also become the source of inhibitions. As we absorb the setting and properties, the same thing must happen with the costumes. We must find ways to adjust our bodies and psychologies so that the costumes become friends and not enemies. Once this ensemble feeling is established with the various production elements, one glance at any of these elements will suffice to rid the actor of any inhibitions associated with them and as a result, make him very much at home in the environment. Such a presence on stage will greatly aid the actor while performing.

Chekhov then speaks in his lecture about establishing the ensemble feeling with the other people on stage. For the ensemble feeling to be established, the actor must find the inner power to be friendly toward everyone regardless of his personal attitude. Each member of the group should make an effort to open himself inwardly, with the greatest possible sincerity, to every other member. The actor should open his heart to these people as if he were among his dearest friends. The actor needs to be ready to receive even the subtlest impressions from every member of the group and be ready to react to these impressions harmoniously.

Chekhov says in the lecture "Ensemble Feeling" that we cannot be comfortable and fully present on stage unless we are friendly with everything, unless a complete ensemble feeling has been established. Not being fully present on stage is another inhibition that is connected with ensemble. It is another way in which we become our own enemies, resulting in uncertainty. However, if the ensemble feeling is established with the setting, properties, costumes and other actors, this uncertainty disappears and the actor becomes more and more present on stage.

Atmosphere and Emotion

Chekhov delved deeply into the notion of atmosphere on the stage. For his system of acting, atmosphere must be carefully chosen by the actors and other artists of the theatre. He states in his lecture "Many-Leveled Acting" that atmosphere is a strong means of expression.[13] In *To the Actor,* Chekhov explains how atmosphere creates a strong bond between the actors and the audience:

> A compelling performance arises out of *reciprocal action* between the actor and the spectator. If the actors, director, author, set designer and, often, the musicians have truly created the atmosphere for the performance, the spectator will not be able to remain aloof from it but will respond with inspiring waves of love and confidence.[14]

In addition, Chekhov contends the atmosphere deepens the perception of the spectators, allowing their feelings to be stirred and awakened. Without atmosphere a spectator will understand the content of the play intellectually. However, with the proper atmosphere the spectator feels the content and very essence of the play and his understanding is broadened by these feelings. As a result, the content of the play becomes richer and more significant. The spectator will perceive a play without atmosphere as a psychologically void space.

Each atmosphere has what Chekhov calls a will of its own. A particular atmosphere's will, its dynamic or driving power, arouses in the actor specific feelings and creative impulses. For example, a happy atmosphere awakens in the actor the desire to expand, extend, open, and spread himself, to burst forth and gain space.[15] On the other hand, an atmosphere of depression or grief will have the opposite effect, causing the actor to feel the urge to contract, close and diminish himself. In some atmospheres the will is not as strong as it is in others but it is always there and influences the actor with as much power as any other atmosphere. Chekhov says, "There is no atmosphere deprived of the inner dynamic, life and will. All you need to get inspiration from it is to open yourself toward it."[16]

In *To the Actor,* Chekhov calls atmospheres "objective feelings," that are very different from the individual feelings of the characters, which he calls "subjective feelings."[17] The example he gives to distinguish the two is that there are usually many different subjective feelings among people watching a car accident, while the accident itself produces a prevailing atmosphere of tragedy, that is, the objective feeling. In his lectures Chekhov uses a different terminology from that in the book. In the lectures, he distinguishes between the general or objective atmosphere of the play and the individual or personal atmosphere of the character.[18] The lectures do not use the word "feelings" in defining atmosphere. Even though it is difficult to separate feelings from atmospheres in Chekhov's scheme of things, I think his terminology in the lectures is clearer. In "Many-Leveled Acting," Chekhov says that one should not confuse a character's individual feelings with atmosphere. A character can keep the same atmosphere throughout a play, while the character's mood and feelings may change several times. Hence, I will use the terms "objective atmosphere" and "individual atmosphere" to explain this concept, and deal separately with the notion of creative feelings.

In the theatre there may be a contrast between the objective atmosphere and the individual atmosphere, but two different objective atmospheres cannot exist simultaneously. A stronger atmosphere will inevitably defeat a weaker one. For example, if there is an objective atmosphere of mystery and tranquility pervading an old abandoned castle and a group of people enters the castle with an objective atmosphere of gaiety, produced by the different individual atmospheres within the group, the two objective atmospheres will clash and one will submit to the other. These aspects of atmospheres provide actors and directors with the means for creating dramatic conflict on stage, for example, the clash between two contrasting atmospheres resulting in the inevitable defeat of one of them, or the clash between the individual atmospheres of the characters and a hostile objective atmosphere resulting in the victory of one over the other. These clashes between contrasts on stage provide suspense and tenseness in the audience, while the resolution of the conflicts provides the audience with an aesthetic satisfaction.

This work with atmospheres is important for any play even if the atmospheres are not clearly stated in the script. Chekhov says that these atmospheres can be created by:

> lights with their shadows and colors; settings with their shapes and forms of compositions; musical and sound effects; groupings of actors, their voices with a variety of timbres, their movements, pauses, changes of tempo, all kinds of rhythmical effects and manner of acting. Practically all that the audience perceives on the stage can serve the purpose of enhancing atmospheres or even creating them anew. [19]

How the actor expresses emotions on stage is complex with any acting system and Chekhov's is no exception. However, he does provide an interesting and useful technique. To understand Chekhov's approach, one needs to examine his statements on the nature of creative feelings that appear in two chapters of *To the Actor* and the comments referred to earlier in his lecture "Love in Our Profession."

Chekhov places great importance on creating feelings in the theatre. As stated earlier in the section on the actor's psychology, Chekhov considers the psychology to be comprised of thoughts, feelings and will. Feelings play an important part in this triad because they modify, control and perfect the other two. A person in real life who is deprived of or neglects his feelings becomes machine-like and has a destructive tendency. There is the same result on stage. A performance without creative feeling is mechanistic. An audience will be cold and untouched by such a performance even if it intellectually understands the content of the play or is able to appreciate the technique and skill of the performances. In real life a person can dispense with feelings for a while, but in the theatre an absence of feelings results in the death of a performance.

Chekhov uses the term "creative feelings" because he distinguishes between feelings in everyday life and the creative feelings an actor uses on stage. I mentioned this distinction earlier when I talked about one of the practical applications of Chekhov's view of human love. As he articulates in his lectures, all creative feelings are based on human love. A creative feeling of hate is based on love, and so the actor enjoys this hating and separates it from the hate he might feel in everyday life. [20]

These creative feelings are unique in other ways as well. They are artistic emotions which are purified of the egotism and personal concerns that exist in everyday emotions. Chekhov contends that everyday emotions are inhibited, insignificant and spoiled by untruths, whereas creative feelings are freeing, significant and artistically true. [21]

Creative feelings have their source in the subconscious. All life experiences accumulate and form the depth of the subconscious. There they are purified of all egotism and become feelings per se. It is from this wealth of purified feelings that the creative individuality gives birth to the psychology of a character. The higher self, which purifies and transforms these feelings, does not cease to exist between performances. It has a continuous life of its own. Even though we are not aware of it, this higher self continually prepares our everyday experiences and feelings for our creative efforts.

In his lecture "Many-Leveled Acting," Chekhov clarifies the relationship between the actor's real life and the actor's art. He says that the acting profession is inseparable from the actor's real, human, private life. This private life affects the actor's art. However, many actors make the mistake of trying to bring this real life onto the stage through naturalistic acting. The problem with this is that such acting makes the performance too primitive and one-dimensional. In its attempt to copy life, such acting becomes too simplistic. [22] Rather it is the subconscious inner activity, which purifies and transforms feelings, that artists should draw upon in their work, not their everyday life experiences. Since this higher self is the vessel for creative activity, it is possible for a creative and talented artist to have an everyday life that is uneventful or insignificant. As an example, Chekhov says,

It is hardly conceivable that Shakespeare, whose everyday life, as far as it is known to us, was so insignificant, and Goethe, whose lot was so placid and contented, drew all their creative ideas from personal experiences only. Indeed, the exterior lives of many lesser literary figures have yielded up far richer biographies than those of the masters, and yet their works will scarcely bear comparison with those of Shakespeare and Goethe. It is the degree of inner activity of the higher self, producing those purified feelings, that is the final determinant of quality in the creations of all artists.[23]

In addition to creative feelings being purified by the higher self, they have two other attributes: they are "unreal" and they are "compassionate." Chekhov explains that these feelings are unreal because they come and go with creative inspiration. If this is not the case, these feelings will stay with the actor, affecting his everyday life, after the performance is over. Such feelings become affected by egotism because they are inseparable from those in everyday life. In addition the use of real feelings on stage makes it impossible for the actor to separate his life from that illusory life of the character. The unreal attribute of creative feelings makes it possible for the actor to enjoy playing villains or other undesirable characters. Using real feelings leads to unhealthy actors, who attempt to squeeze their everyday feelings out of themselves on stage. Creative feelings are compassionate in the sense that they allow an actor to penetrate the psychology of the character and have compassion for the character while performing. Chekhov says, "Thus, the true artist in you is able to suffer for Hamlet, cry with Juliet, laugh about the mischief-making of Falstaff."[24]

Chekhov's notion of creative feelings is very similar to Susanne Langer's notion of the feelings a musician uses in performance. In her discussion of "utterance" in *Feeling and Form*, Langer talks about the values and dangers of personal feelings for the performing musician. Here Langer deals with the singer and instrumentalist. She never makes similar statements about the actor, but her ideas about feelings in performance seem to apply to the actor, as much as they do to the musician and vocalist.

Langer claims that if the artist's personal feelings are concentrated on the content or significance of the artwork, these feelings become the dynamic force of the artwork.[25] Even though this dynamic force seems like everyday emotion, it is really a unique emotion that exists apart from everyday concerns. Langer claims that there is a danger involved with the use of personal feelings. When the artist makes the performance only an outlet for his personal emotions, the performance is an emotional catharsis for the artist. This artist will perform passionately, but the artwork's expressive forms will be inarticulate and blurred. Hence, for Langer and Chekhov personal emotions are necessary for the artist, but these emotions must be unique. They must be different from those emotions the artist experiences in everyday life, which are confused and formless in performance. These emotions must be artistic ones, which are indigenous to the artwork and possess clear artistic form.

Langer goes a step further by saying that the artist does not have to experience every emotion that he conveys in performance.[26] She contends that every artist has a personal repertoire of pieces that he is able to play. These pieces, or roles for the actor, involve emotions that are within the artist's emotional knowledge or awareness. However, the artist does not have to express only those feelings he has experienced in everyday life. The feelings expressed must be possible for the artist to imagine. For Langer, it is the possibility of imagining these feelings that is more important for the artist than the actual experiencing of these feelings in everyday life. This concept relates directly to Chekhov's claim that the actor is not limited to expressing only those emotions he has experienced in everyday life. Instead, the actor expresses those creative emotions that are produced by his higher self.

Now that we understand Chekhov's notion of creative feelings, it is important to examine how these emotions are used on stage. Chekhov says that one's individual feelings are impossible to command directly, that is, an actor cannot order himself to feel any particular emotion. When actors pretend they are feeling a certain emotion on stage, they often try to squeeze these feelings out of themselves. These attempts are usually unsuccessful, and when they are successful, it is usually by accident, not a result of technical skill. According to Chekhov, "True artistic feelings, if they refuse to appear by themselves, must be coaxed by some technical means which will make an actor the master over them."[27]

Imagination and atmosphere are two ways to coax feelings by technical means. Chekhov's third suggestion is to coax them by the use of qualities. A simple physical gesture, the raising of an arm for instance, is easy to perform because it is within one's will to do so. If you add a quality, for example, caution, to this movement the movement is just as easy to make but now it is no longer just a physical action. This physical action has acquired a psychological nuance, that is, a sensation of caution that permeates the movement. It would be just as easy to move the entire body with the same quality and as a result, the entire body would be filled with this sensation. Chekhov says, "Sensation is the vessel into which your genuine artistic feelings pour easily and by themselves; it is a kind of magnet which draws to it feelings and emotions akin to whatever quality you have chosen for your movement."[28]

As a result of this approach to feelings, actors do not have to order themselves to feel a specific emotion. The simple process of moving with a specific quality creates a sensation of the emotion, through which actors' feelings are aroused. Repeating the movement causes the feelings to become stronger and opens one up to the whole gamut of emotions and nuances of feelings that are related to that quality. In addition, this same technique can be applied when the actor is in a static position. Feelings are aroused just as strongly when one stands, sits or lies with a quality as they are when one moves with this quality. Chekhov cautions that it may not always be easy to choose the correct quality for a particular scene. If actors are indecisive about the correct quality, they should try several qualities until they settle on the one that works best. Applying more than one quality at a time can also work because they may merge into one sensation that will produce the feelings needed.

As an exercise for this work with qualities, Chekhov suggests that the actor perform movements or simple business several times until the movement can be made with ease. Then a quality is added and the movement repeated until the sensation fills the entire body and the feelings respond to it. Chekhov cautions not to force the feelings or hurry the result. Next, the actor can add words to the movement or work through improvisations with partners following the same procedure. These exercises will help the actor technically to master feelings and strengthen the bond between the actor's body and psychology.

Eddie Grove, a teacher of Chekhov's acting system, uses qualities in interesting ways. He sets up brief improvisations, giving actors only one line and a quality. The qualities lead the actors to intentions and relationships, as they create emotional given circumstances for the actors' feelings. Grove instructs the actors to perform these small scenes quickly and then builds longer improvisations with these scenes as a structure. While the actors are working with these improvisations, Grove tells them that their entire psychologies will work for them if they create the proper stimuli and give their thoughts, feelings and will a chance to work. The use of qualities allows this to happen and keeps emotional expression within the control of the actors.

Blair Cutting, who worked with Chekhov at Dartington Hall and at Ridgefield, taught at The Michael Chekhov Studio until his death in 1983. Cutting also set up short scenes with qualities, but he gave each actor two lines, instead of one, taken from grade B movies he directed. Each actor was also given a quality that guided him during the improvisation. Cutting also used quality walks. While walking around the space, the actors were given several different qualities, one at a time. They changed their physical movements instantly from one quality to another. As the actors walked with each quality, they also concentrated on placing their centers in various places and radiating their energies from these centers.

The ability to change instantly from one quality to another gives actors the ability to change quickly from one emotional expression to another. Because the technique circumvents trying to feel the emotion first, and lets qualities coax the emotions, the actor remains in control and the emotions are strong without being forced.

It seems to me that this technique is extremely valuable because the creative emotions expressed by the use of qualities appear to be true emotions but are not the actors' real-life emotions. In addition, the actors remain in control of these emotions are not overcome or ruled by them, which often happens when actors try to squeeze their real emotions out of themselves.

Psychological Gesture

The psychological gesture is one of the most unique and useful aspects of Chekhov's system of acting. As I talk with theatre people about Chekhov, they may not know much about his acting system but they are usually familiar with the term psychological gesture. It is one of those unique characteristics, like Stanislavsky's emotion memory, that has implanted Chekhov in the minds of many. Unfortunately, also like Stanislavsky's emotion memory, it is often misunderstood and thought of as the nucleus of the Chekhov system. Regardless of the uniqueness, and what I perceive as the brilliance of the psychological gesture, it is in essence only one part of the actor's technique in Chekhov's complex acting system.

As the use of qualities and sensations is the key to the actor's creative feelings, psychological gesture is the key to another part of the actor's psychology, the desires or will power. Like feelings, the will power of the actor cannot be commanded. It also must be coaxed by indirect means. Chekhov says that if you perform a strong, well-shaped gesture and repeat it several times, your will power becomes stronger and stronger under the influence of the gesture. The kind of movement you perform will give your will power a certain direction or inclination and awaken in you a definite desire, want or wish. Relating this process to the work with qualities, Chekhov says, "So we may say that the *strength* of the movement stirs our will power in general; the *kind* of movement awakens in us a definite corresponding *desire,* and the *quality* of the same movement conjures up our *feelings.*"[29]

Chekhov provides several examples of the psychological gesture, and the illustrations in *To the Actor* by Nicolai Remisoff are good complements to these examples. For the purposes of clarity, I recount one of the examples here:

> Imagine you are playing a character which, according to your first general impression, has a *strong* and unbending *will*, is possessed by dominating, despotic *desires,* and is filled with *hatred* and *disgust.*
>
> You look for a suitable over-all gesture which can express all this in the character, and perhaps after a few attempts you find it (see Drawing 1).
>
> It is strong and well shaped. When repeated several times it will tend to strengthen your will. The direction of each limb, the final position of the whole body as well as the

inclination of the head are such that they are bound to call up a *definite desire* for *domination* and *despotic* conduct. The *qualities* which fill and permeate each muscle of the entire body, will provoke within you feelings of *hatred* and *disgust*. Thus, through the psychological gesture, you penetrate and stimulate the depths of your own psychology.[30]

Chekhov chooses the term psychological gesture because of the effect it has on the actor: it affects the entire psychology and its purpose is to influence, stir, mold and attune the actor's whole inner life to its artistic aims and purposes.[31]

The psychological gesture is a preparatory tool that is never shown to the audience. It is not a gesture that a character uses on stage. This has caused some confusion in the minds of theatre people who have heard of the term but have never read Chekhov's description of it or worked with it themselves. The term itself is responsible for some of this confusion. In many plays there are characters, like Gayeff in *The Cherry Orchard,* who have a characteristic gesture that reveals something about their psychology. Throughout the play, Gayeff moves his hands and body as if he were playing billiards. This type of characteristic gesture is called by some a psychological gesture because it is a repetitive gesture that tells the audience something about the psychology of Gayeff. However, it is totally different from Chekhov's concept of psychological gesture. With Chekhov the psychological gesture is a technique for developing the actor's psychology and its responsiveness to the body, as well as a technique for developing a characterization. It is never a gesture that is performed for an audience.

In discussing the way an actor applies the psychological gesture to his work, Chekhov begins by discussing an alternative: using one's analytical mind instead of the psychological gesture. He claims that relying on the reasoning mind first is a difficult and laborious process because the mind is too cold and abstract to be able to develop an artistic work. In fact, relying on your mind at first can even weaken and retard one's ability to act. Knowing intellectually what the feelings and desires of a character are does not enable one to fulfill these desires or experience the feelings on stage. This does not mean that one discounts the mind altogether, but one should not appeal to it at first. Instead, it should remain in the background so that it will not hamper one's creative efforts. Chekhov clarifies this by saying, "Of course, your mind can and will be very helpful to you in evaluating, correcting, verifying, making additions and offering suggestions, *but it should not do all these before your creative intuition has asserted itself and spoken fully.*"[32]

As an alternative, the psychological gesture allows you to appeal to your creative forces directly. You appeal to your entire psychology, which of course includes the mind but also involves feelings and desires. Very little, if any, intellectualizing is needed to discover the proper psychological gesture for a character. From a first reading of the play, you get some idea of what the character is through your intuition and creative imagination. For example, if you ask yourself what the main desire of the character might be, you will get some answer, regardless of how vague at first, which will act as a springboard for the psychological gesture.

Once you have done this, Chekhov suggests that you begin with only the hands and arms and explore different gestures that fit your initial impression. It is important to remember that the gesture needs to be strong and well-defined. You pay great attention to detail and slight changes of movement and position for the hands and arms as you work. Then the gesture is expanded to include the entire body, and after this complete gesture is explored, you will know whether your initial impression of the character was correct. If you are not satisfied with this gesture, start again with a new impression of the character and repeat the same process. You keep working with the psychological gesture, always refining and perfecting it, until it seems right to you.

Psychological gesture (PG) is thus a means of character investigation. It is also, according to Chekhov, a means to a greater end:

> By using the PG as a means of exploiting the character, you actually do more than that. You prepare yourself for acting it. By elaborating, improving, perfecting and exercising the PG you are, more and more, becoming the very character yourself at the same time. Your will, your feelings are stirred and awakened in you. The more you progress in this work, the more the PG reveals to you the entire character in *condensed* form, making you the possessor and master of its *unchangeable core.*[33]

Hence, you are discovering the essence of the part from the beginning of your preparation, which then makes it easier and more profitable to work out the details on stage.

It is also possible to use the psychological gesture for any moment the character has on stage. A psychological gesture might be successfully developed for a scene, a speech or even a sentence that needs special attention. No one can tell the actor whether or not the psychological gesture is right for a particular role. A director may make suggestions, but the actor is the only one who can decide ultimately if the gesture works for the character.

The only criterion for judging the psychological gesture is making sure one has followed the necessary conditions. Some of these conditions have already been alluded to. They are:

1. It must be an archetypal gesture.
2. It must be strong but without unnecessary muscular tension.
3. It must be as simple as possible.
4. It must have a clear and definite form.
5. It must be performed in the correct tempo.
6. It must be radiated beyond the boundaries of your own body.[34]

Those conditions that require the gesture to be simple, clear, definite and radiate beyond the boundaries of the body are self-explanatory based on what I have said so far about Chekhov's use of the gesture. Radiation is used here as it was described earlier in the section on the actor's body and psychology. However, I think the other conditions require further explanation.

Chekhov best describes archetypal gesture in terms of what it is not. It is not the type of gesture that actors use on stage or in everyday life. In other words, it is not a "realistic" gesture. It is a gesture that serves as a model for all possible gestures of the same kind. It seems to me that this archetypal gesture is similar to the abstract gesture one uses when working on sound-and-movement exercises, like those developed and used by the Open Theatre. In fact, although I have not been able to make a clear connection between the two, psychological gesture seems to be a natural forerunner of sound-and-movement.

Sound-and-movement technique, as developed by Joseph Chaikin at the Open Theatre, requires the actor to perform a simple, well-defined action with the voice and body. This is an impulsive action and a pure action that is not representative of everyday behavior.[35] This technique is an outgrowth of the physical adjustment work of Nola Chilton, a teacher of the Stanislavsky method. Chilton uses her principle of physical adjustment as a means to help actors deal with non-naturalistic material. It is a way to help them approach parts in plays where the character is not organized according to the principles of psychology.[36] Chaikin's purpose was to free his actors to develop means of expression that went beyond everyday gestures and vocal patterns, to help the actors be more expressive of their psychologies and to develop an ensemble. Sound-and-movement was only one technique for achieving these aims but it became the cornerstone of the work done at the Open Theatre. Its similarities to psychological gesture are striking.

The fact that the psychological gesture must be strong but without unnecessary tension is an important point. It emphasizes Chekhov's earlier point that the actor must perform everything with a feeling of ease. Many actors have a tendency to strain and use all of their muscular power while performing a strong gesture. But Chekhov contends that such straining or any unnecessary tension actually weakens the gesture or movement instead of strengthening it. A violent psychological gesture needs to have muscular strength, but the real power of such a gesture is more psychological than physical. Chekhov's example to illustrate this point is that a mother will hug her child with great maternal strength but her muscles are almost completely relaxed.

Tempo may also be misunderstood as it relates to psychological gesture. Characters in plays, as well as people in everyday life, live in different tempos. The character's tempo depends upon the actor's interpretation of the role, and the actor needs to be aware of this when preparing the psychological gesture. The same psychological gesture performed at different tempos will have different effects on the actor. As a result, tempo is an important consideration in developing the psychological gesture. Chekhov says that, "Our usual conception of tempo on the stage fails to distinguish between the *inner* and *outer* varieties."[37] His inner tempo deals with the speed of changes of the different parts of the psychology, while the outer tempo is expressed in either quick or slow actions and speech. Chekhov encourages actors to take advantage of contrasting inner and outer tempos with their characters. A character's thoughts, feelings and desires may be changing in quick succession, while the voice and body are calm and slow. Both inner and outer slow tempos can be used effectively, but the actor must always remain active. To use a slow tempo does not mean to be passive on stage. By the same token, a fast tempo should never cause the actor to rush or use unnecessary psychological and physical tension. As Chekhov states in his lecture "Monotony," changes in tempos are a good way to take advantage of changes in the character, and thus avoid monotony or uniformity.[38] Chekhov suggests that the actor try the beginning and end of the play in different tempos.

In order to understand and appreciate fully Chekhov's techniques of creative expression, one must accept his premise that great acting comes from the actor's imagination. There is little here to benefit an actor who wants a lucid technique for translating real-life people into characters for the stage. If, in addition, the actor is primarily interested in line readings and blocking that are decided upon early in the rehearsal process, he will be frustrated by Chekhov's techniques. Atmosphere, creative feelings and psychological gesture require time and patience. They are not easily defined and their results are often unclear at first. I do not think these techniques are good for all actors, especially those who are practically minded and who need things to be understandable at all times. However, for actors who enjoy exploring the depths of creative expression, whose imaginations love to improvise as they create characters who are not tied to real-life prototypes, Chekhov provides indispensable keys to success.

6

Keys to Transformation

Character, Characterization, and Individuality

Chekhov's ideas concerning character and characterization, included in chapter 6 of *To the Actor,* are amplified considerably in a two-part lecture entitled "Characterization." His basic premise is that "every true artist, and especially a talented actor, bears within himself a deeply rooted and often unconscious desire for transformation; speaking our theatrical language, a desire for characterization."[1] In developing characters fully, one must distinguish the individual characteristics within types of characters. We see many different types of people in everyday life, as we see many different types of characters on the stage. Many actors are satisfied with merely playing one of these types. But an actor should be aware of variations and the individual characteristics the playwright provides. The individuality of the character should be the actor's focus and not the type of person to which the individual might belong.

Many actors are prone to play all their roles as "straight" parts; they play all their characters as themselves in real life. According to Chekhov, there is no such thing as a "straight" part. As stated earlier, Chekhov sees the role of the actor as one who interprets life, and not as one who merely shows life as it is. He feels that an actor who only plays himself on stage is like a painter who always paints self-portraits. Such acting also has a negative effect on one's ability to perform well, by causing talent to degenerate. It creates theatrical habits and worn-out clichés.

Recognizing the differences among individual characters is a starting point for the actor, because the first thing the actor should do is discover how the character is different from himself. To do this the actor should ask himself three questions: What is the difference between my way of thinking and the character's? What is the difference between the feelings and emotions of the character and myself? What is the difference between the will of the character and my own will?[2] By doing this the actor discovers the differences between his psychology and the character's psychology. The character might think slower or faster than the actor; he might be cold in his feelings while the actor is passionate; he might have a weak will as opposed to the strong will of the actor. The more differences the actor finds, the clearer and more distinct the character will become, and the actor's understanding of the character will be improved.

The actor should write down all of the differences discovered and with them in mind go over the entire part and allow the characteristics of the character to creep into the actor's performance. Chekhov cautions not to force an immediate result or toil over this process. If it is done playfully and easily, the results will come by themselves. This technique of approaching a part will keep the actor within the type of character being played, but will allow the actor to go through a transformation and express the character's individuality.

Chekhov suggests that the actor physically express the character's individuality by finding an imaginary body for the character. As soon as the actor has some idea of the characteristics of the character, he imagines what kind of body the character might have. The actor observes this image for a while and then imagines that his body and the character's body meet in the same space. This meeting in space of the actor's own body and the character's body is what Chekhov calls the imaginary body of the character. The actor imagines that he steps into this body, or puts it on like a costume in a masquerade. The result is that not only does the actor find a physical expression for the character, but the actor's psychology is changed as well. Chekhov says that in everyday life when one puts on the clothes of another person in a masquerade, these different clothes make a person feel and think differently. A similar thing happens with the imaginary body, but the result is much stronger because:

> This assumption of the character's imaginary physical form influences your psychology ten times more strongly than any garment. The imaginary body stands, as it were, *between* your real body and your psychology, influencing both of them with equal force. Step by step, you begin to move, speak and feel in accord with it; that is to say, your character now dwells within you (or, if you prefer, you dwell within it).[3]

Chekhov's concept of imaginary body is more than a means of finding a physical expression for the character. As he says in the above statement, it also has a strong effect on the psychology. As a result, the imaginary body helps the actor totally transform himself into the character. In a sense, the imaginary body is a meeting point between the actor and the character arrived at through the actor's imagination. This result cannot be achieved as fully through the mind alone. An intellectual analysis of the character does not spark the actor's feelings and will in the way the imagination does. The actor should not exaggerate the physical qualities produced by the imaginary body, but should use his artistic sense to guide the incorporation of these qualities into the character.

The same result can be achieved if the actor begins with imagining only part of the character's body instead of the whole thing at once. For example, the actor may begin by imagining the character's neck or arms, and then continue the process until the entire body is incorporated. Chekhov emphasizes that there are no rules governing this process.[4] The actor should be guided by what works best and his own artistic taste.

This work with the imaginary body can be enriched if the actor adds to it Chekhov's concept of imaginary center. This idea was touched on briefly in the earlier chapter on the actor's body and psychology. Chekhov contends that as long as the actor's center remains in the chest, as in his earlier exercise, the actor feels in a neutral state. But when the center shifts to another part of the body or even outside the body, the actor's psychology and physicality will change.

In the first part of his lecture on characterization, Chekhov says that everyone in real life and every character created for the stage has a psycho-physical center. By observing people in everyday life and using the imagination, one can find where this center exists in different people. For example, a conceited person may have a center in a raised eyebrow or in a frozen smile. The center may exist outside the body, as with a cowardly person's center hanging in the air beneath his buttocks.[5] Locating these various centers is one way of recognizing the differences between ourselves and others, thus helping to develop the individuality of our characters.

This imaginary center also has a certain quality that must be added to the actor's use of it. Two centers placed in the same spot will have entirely different results if they are given different qualities. For example, a center in the head of a character given the qualities of big, shining and radiating will suggest a wise person. However, a center in the same place with small, tense and hard qualities will suggest a stupid or narrow-minded person.[6] Depending on the character being played, the center may be either static or movable. A character who is bewildered or intoxicated might best be expressed by a movable center. The actor's imagination must be free to develop the centers and qualities that seem to work best for the individual character. There are no rules as to where to locate the center of a character or what quality that center should have.

To develop this ability to find the imaginary center, the actor should observe people from everyday life and characters from plays, and decide what imaginary centers and qualities might best be suited for these people. The actor should never ask anyone if his impression is correct, but should trust his own judgment, intuition and talent. This technique, as well as most of

Chekhov's techniques, works best when the actor approaches it with a sense of play, as a child plays at becoming different characters. This sense of play does not mean that the actor is lazy or does not take the work seriously. It means that the actor does not labor over the process, but has the freedom to let the imagination and intuition work creatively.

In *To the Actor,* Chekhov defines characterization as a peculiar feature that is indigenous to the character.[7] This characterization acts as a finishing touch to the character and must spring from the character as a whole. As an example of characterization, Chekhov says that:

> An absent-minded character, while holding a conversation with another person, could show a characteristic manner of quickly blinking his eyes, at the same time directing a finger-pointing gesture at his interlocutor and pausing with mouth slightly ajar before he collects his thoughts and puts them into words.[8]

Chekhov suggests that, as with the character as a whole, the actor find suggestions for characterizations by observing people in everyday life. However, one must remember that the actor is not merely copying life, and so these observations must follow or be accompanied by the use of the creative imagination. In other words, the actor should see what the imagination suggests about applying observations to a character or characterization, instead of mechanically copying the observation while developing the character.

In his lectures on characterization, Chekhov makes important points about this process that are not mentioned in *To the Actor.* First, he suggests a method of approaching a character that is not mentioned in the book. With this method, the actor begins by making a list of all the business the character is going to perform in the play. This list must be detailed and specific. The actor then begins to perform this business in the proper sequence with his entire concentration on how it is being performed. The actor must take into consideration the given circumstances and what impressions he has about the character, but the focus is on the "how" of the character's actions. In addition to discovering how the action can be performed and the differences in how it is performed under changing given circumstances, the actor will become more familiar with the character as a whole. This technique is another method of digging deeply into the character and finding its essence, because the physical behavior of the character will tell the actor much about the character's psychology.

In the second part of the characterization lecture, Chekhov explains the actor's mask, a concept that expands his method of developing a character. He begins by saying that there are two psychological processes that interest actors in their desire for transformation: to express themselves on stage and to absorb and accumulate life experiences and all sorts of knowledge.[9] According to Chekhov, as actors' experiences and knowledge become richer, their expression on stage becomes more colorful. He compares this process to breathing. The accumulation of experiences and knowledge equals inhaling and the expression on stage equals exhaling.

However, since actors never express themselves directly on stage, they need a character mask to serve as a conduit for their creative expression. This mask is developed through a process of transformation. Without the mask, actors are portraying themselves as in real life and, as a result, leave the frame of art. Use of the character mask allows actors to transform themselves and express their creative individuality through the characters they are playing. In everyday life a mask provides people with a way of hiding their true feelings, but on stage the character mask is a way of expressing true feelings through characters—or as Chekhov might put it, exhaling on stage.

The process of inhaling requires an actor to develop the ability to open himself to people and events while observing them so that this observation permeates the actor with the qualities of these real-life phenomena. For example, while observing, the actor should not just stare at a person, but open himself to that person and penetrate the person's psychology. This process applies to other types of observation as well. Pictures of people from different historical periods or even cartoons and caricatures are useful objects of observation and should be approached in the same way.

"Creative individuality" is another important term in Chekhov's acting system. On the surface the term refers to the unique way an artist expresses himself, but the term is extremely complex because it contains Chekhov's notion of the actor's "higher self." In the second part of his lecture on characterization, Chekhov says that it is not the person in everyday life who wants to transform himself on stage, but another self beyond the threshold of our consciousness.[10] This self is the attitude we take toward life, events and other people; it is different from the self that glides through life. This other self remains hidden until we explore it as artists. When working on a character we must discover the attitudes of this other self toward the character. Chekhov says that this is our "higher self." It is the true artist in us, the bearer of our talent, the creator of all our roles.

In moments of creative inspiration, the everyday "I" of the actor undergoes a kind of metamorphosis into the "higher I" or "higher self" described above. This "higher I" uses the actor's emotions, voice and body as building materials to create the character. It takes possession of these materials and causes the actor to feel as if he were standing above these materials and the everyday self. While creating the character, the actor is aware of both the everyday "I" and the "higher I" existing simultaneously.

> Once the higher self has that building material well in hand, it begins to mold it from within; it moves your body, making it flexible, sensitive and receptive to all creative impulses; it speaks with your voice, stirs your imagination and increases your inner activity. Moreover, it grants you genuine feelings, makes you original and inventive, awakens and maintains your ability to improvise. In short, it puts you in a *creative* state. You begin to act under its inspiration. Everything you do on the stage now surprises you as well as your audience; all seems entirely new and unexpected. Your impression is that it is happening spontaneously and that you do nothing but serve as its medium of expression.[11]

To effectively use this "higher I" on stage, one must remember that it works hand-in-hand with the actor's lower self. The actor's everyday consciousness acts as a controlling force to see that the higher consciousness does not get out of hand. The business of the character, its relationship with the other characters and the psychological patterns of development of the character must be carried out as established in rehearsal. The everyday consciousness makes sure that the higher consciousness acts within the boundaries that are fixed for the performance. When this happens, the performance is a result of the cooperation between the "higher I" and the "lower I."

There is a third consciousness that exists in this process. It is the consciousness of the character as created by the actor. Even though the character is a fictive being, it has its own life and its own independent "I." It is a consciousness that is created by the actor's creative individuality during performance.

As I stated in chapter 1, this concept of the "higher I" seems to be closely linked to Chekhov's belief in Anthroposophy. While discussing his views about one's ability to know Christ in a higher state of consciousness, Chekhov calls this consciousness the "higher I."[12] To my knowledge, Chekhov never said that his notion of the "higher I" included in his acting system came from his religious views. However, it seems to me that the similarities are so striking that his acting system must have been affected by this religious concept. The connection does not necessarily make acting a religious experience, but it does admit that the higher state of consciousness reached when one knows Christ is similar to the higher state of consciousness reached by actors when they are creatively inspired.

In addition, as the monks who practiced hesychasm had a technique for reaching their higher state of consciousness in which they communed with Christ, Chekhov's entire acting system is a technique for reaching creative inspiration, in which the actor's "lower I" is transformed into the "higher I." As John Dehner pointed out, with Chekhov's acting system you do not wait for inspiration to magically appear. Instead, inspiration appears as an end result of the practicing of Chekhov's techniques and exercises.[13] As you can coax your feelings by technical means, for example, the use of qualities, you can also coax inspiration through an awareness of creative individuality.

In addition to including Chekhov's notion of the "higher I," creative individuality also unites the actor with the audience. Creative individuality's ubiquitous nature extends itself to serve as a spectator for the character it creates. Chekhov explains this by saying:

> From the other side of the footlights it [creative individuality] follows the spectators' experiences, shares their enthusiasm, excitement and disappointments. More than that, it has the ability to foretell audience reaction an instant before it takes place. It knows what will satisfy the spectator, what will inflame him and what will leave him cold. Thus, for the actor with an awakened awareness of his higher *I*, the audience is a link which connects him as an artist with the desires of his contemporaries. [14]

Throughout his career, and especially at the Moscow Art Theatre, the First Studio and Dartington Hall, Chekhov had continually explored the actor-audience relationship. One unique aim of the Dartington Studio, for instance, was to relate the work of the studio to the sociological problems of the time. Chekhov's "creative individuality" not only links the actor and audience during performance, but it also links the actor to the private lives of the audience members. Chekhov says, "Listening to the 'voice' speaking to him from the audience during the performance, he [the actor] slowly begins to relate himself to the world and his brothers. He acquires a new 'organ' which connects him with life outside the theatre and awakens his contemporary responsibilities." [15]

In his lecture "Many-Leveled Acting," Chekhov explains how this connection with the audience existed in his own work. For several performances of *Hamlet* at the Second Moscow Art Theatre, Chekhov performed before selected audiences, each one comprised of a specific type of person. [16] For each audience, he performed the role of Hamlet differently; for example, he performed differently for the audience of sophisticated professionals than he did for the audience of simple workers. Many nuances of the performance were different for each audience, but it was not the result of an intellectual choice to make changes in the performance. Chekhov said that it was his higher self that directed him to respond to each audience differently. His higher self developed a deep bond between himself and the audience. It provided for a collaboration with the audience without being subservient or egotistical. Chekhov later discovered the same thing happening with audiences composed of different types of people. With these mixed audiences the bond was just as strong but the changes in the performance were more varied. He felt himself responding differently to different parts of the house, depending on who was sitting where. Chekhov emphasized that these experiences did not come from a mental process, but came from his higher self. They were the result of his creative individuality functioning in his performances.

Different Approaches for Different Roles

Once an actor has found the keys to transforming himself into a character, the performance must be fine-tuned. Such refinement is achieved through Chekhov's notion of the composition of a performance, which applies laws of musical composition to the art of acting. How the actor and director approach this composition is determined by the type of play being done and how the director is approaching the production. As I have pointed out before, allusions to music are an important part of Chekhov's acting system. He quotes W. Paret's statement, "Each art constantly strives to resemble music."[17] Not all of Chekhov's laws of composition are musical terms, but they all appear to have a direct connection to Chekhov's claim that a dramatic performance should be composed like a symphony. Chekhov's purpose is to make the actor aware of how a performance should be structured and to develop in the actor the director's all-embracing view of the performance as a whole.

Chekhov discusses seven laws of composition for performance and the creation of characters. To illustrate these laws of composition, Chekhov uses examples from *King Lear*. His first law of composition is the law of triplicity. Chekhov says that in every good play there is a battle between good and evil which is the driving force of the play. In every play, no matter how complex its construction, the plot can be divided into three sections that follow the beginning, development and conclusion of the driving force.

The laws of polarity and transformation are closely connected to this law of triplicity. The law of polarity dictates that the beginning and end of a performance should be polar to one another, and the process that transforms the beginning to its opposite at the end is called the law of transformation. Chekhov says that obeying these first three laws will enrich the performance in many ways beyond providing beauty and harmony.

Polarity's importance stems from the fact that we understand and experience things differently when we see them in light of true contrasts. Art mirrors life in the sense that our evaluation and understanding of life experiences are different when viewed in the light of true contrasts. For example, we examine life in terms of death, good as it relates to evil, happiness in relation to unhappiness. An audience has a similar experience when viewing polarity on stage. Chekhov says, "Contrast between the beginning and the end is truly the quintessential of a well-composed performance."[18] The contrasting beginning and end of a performance explain and complement each other through the power of their contrast. Our sense of polarity conjures up a vision of the beginning of the performance as well watch the end.

The means by which the polarity is expressed is up to the director and his collaborators. Music, scenery, costumes and lighting all need to be well coordinated to establish the proper atmosphere for the beginning and a contrasting atmosphere for the end. The director might have the actors take advantage of contrasting tempos to express this polarity in the performances. He might also use a different type of contrast through the juxtaposition of two major characters. In Chekhov's example from *King Lear*, Edmond and Lear are contrasted to each other and are polar in the way they are seen individually at the beginning and end of the play.

Chekhov's law of transformation posits a continuous process that can be seen in any moment of a production as this moment relates to the beginning and end. Keep in mind that Chekhov is talking about the transformation of the beginning into its opposite at the end. Each moment of the play between the beginning and the end is involved in this transformation process. Each moment evolves from the preceding moment into the next moment. Explaining the benefits derived from being aware of this process, Chekhov says:

> Bearing in mind how all the scenes transform one into the other under the influence of the three laws of composition, the director and actors can easily distinguish between the important and the unimportant, between the major and the minor. They will be able to follow the basic line of the play and the battle raging in it without getting lost in the details. Seen in the light of composition, the scenes themselves will prompt the director as to how they should best be staged, because their significance to the whole play is unmistakably revealed to him.[19]

Chekhov's fourth law of composition involves the finding of climaxes for the three big sections mentioned in his law of triplicity. Each of the three units has its own characteristic qualities and prevailing powers of various strengths. The moments of maximum tension within these units are called climaxes. There are three climaxes, one for each unit, which are regulated by the laws of triplicity, polarity and transformation. These three climaxes are related to each other and to the three units in the following way: "The climax of the first unit is a kind of summary of the plot thus far; the second climax also shows in condensed form how the plot of the second or middle unit develops, and the third climax crystallizes the finale of the plot within the framework of the last unit."[20]

Chekhov stresses that these three main climaxes should be found by artistic intuition rather than by reasoning. When discovered by this process, they provide the key to the main idea and to the basic dynamic of the play. In addition, each climax expresses the essence of its own unit. Each of the three units can also be divided into smaller units, each with its own climax called an auxiliary climax.

Chekhov makes an interesting suggestion to directors about the sequencing of rehearsals. He says it is unfortunate that habit forces directors to begin rehearsals with the beginning of the play and then proceed rehearsing the scenes of the play in chronological order. As an alternative, he suggests that the director start rehearsing with the scenes that include the three main climaxes. If the whole play is vivid in the imagination of the director, it is better to begin with the scenes that express the gist of the play and then rehearse scenes of lesser importance. For example, after rehearsing the three main climaxes, the director might rehearse the auxiliary climaxes and proceed from there.

In two of his lectures, Chekhov elaborates on this point.[21] He claims that rehearsing from the beginning to the end helps to produce stale and mechanical performances. It produces productions that are sometimes accurate but not inspired. His suggestion is to break up the sequence by beginning with the scenes that are most important, and then proceeding to other scenes in order of their importance. In the case of a short rehearsal period, it is beneficial to work first on the scenes that are the most difficult and then spend what time you can on the other scenes.

The fifth law of composition deals with what Chekhov terms accents, those moments of lesser tension in the play that are not included in the main and auxiliary climaxes. An accent may be a pause, a line, a speech or several speeches in sequence that are not defined as one of the climaxes. Accents are important from the point of view of composition. For example, an accent can contain the impulse for an ensuing scene, or summarize a scene that has just occurred. It can clarify a climax by preceding or directly following the climax. Chekhov suggests that after a director rehearses the main and auxiliary climaxes, he should proceed with the accidents.

Chekhov's sixth law of composition is the law of rhythmical repetitions. He suggests that there are many ways in which this law is manifested in the universe, but there are only two such manifestations that are important for the theatre: "First, when phenomena repeat themselves regularly in space or time, or both, and remain unchanged; second, when phenomena change with each successive repetition."[22]

Each kind of repetition evokes different reactions in the spectator. In the first, where things remain unchanged, the spectator gets the impression of eternity or endlessness, depending on whether the repetition occurs in time or space. This kind of repetition is used often on stage to create a specific atmosphere, for example, the rhythmical sound of a bell or clock or the visual repetition of rows of windows or pillars in the setting. Rhythmical movements of actors or the rhythmical appearance and disappearance of actors can also create a specific atmosphere that makes use of this kind of repetition.

The effect produced by the second kind of repetition, where phenomena change with each repetition, is quite different. It will either increase or diminish certain impressions the spectator gets from the production. These impressions could include the perception of a character, the mood or tone of the play, relationships within the play, etc. Chekhov gives several examples of this kind of repetition. His first example deals with the repetition of the kingly theme in *King Lear*. He says that at three points in the play the kingly theme appears strongly. At the first point, we see Lear as a powerful earthly king, resulting in the image of a pompous tyrant being implanted in the spectator's mind. The second appearance of this theme is in the fourth act where Lear appears mad. The spectator's impression of Lear is changed considerably as the repetition emphasizes the decline of the earthly king and the rise of the spiritual king. This impression of Lear is supported by the entire visual image: his torn clothes, the locale of the scene, Lear's behavior, etc. At the end of the play occurs the third point when this theme is repeated. Lear appears with his dead daughter and then dies himself. This repetition is the final step in showing the death of the earthly king and the immortality of the spiritual king. This point of the play is made clear by the law of rhythmical repetitions. As Chekhov says:

> Hence the repetition of the "King" theme serves to increase the spiritual meaning of the "King" concept. This rhythmical repetition again reveals to us one of the aspects of the main idea of the tragedy: "The King," *the higher self in man, has the power to live and grow and transform itself under the blows of ruthless destiny, and is able to transcend the boundaries of physical death.*[23]

Chekhov's last law of composition is the law of rhythmical waves. He says that the manifestations of life do not follow a straight line but undulate like waves, breathing rhythmically. These waves change with each different phenomenon. The same thing happens on stage when one considers inner and outer action. A well-executed pause, filled with purpose, is what Chekhov calls inner action. It is a moment that has its significance implied by silence. The opposite of this is outer action, where all visible and audible means are used to the fullest extent. Between these extremes there is an entire spectrum of outer action that is less perceptible and often resembles a pause. The rhythmical waves of a performance are the undulation of the inner and outer action.

A performance should be filled with a variety of rhythmical waves. Chekhov says that these waves give a performance life and make it beautiful and expressive without getting monotonous. He says that some directors make the mistake of assuming a performance must either build to a crescendo at the end of the play or build to a climax somewhere in the middle of the play. However, if the director realizes that there are many climaxes within a play, and many rhythmical waves to be expressed, the performance will have much more power and variety.

Chekhov's laws of composition also include the composition of characters. Each character has specific psychological traits that are the foundation of the character's composition. As a result, the director must make sure that the differences between characters are emphasized but that the characters complement each other as much as possible. To do this the director and actors must determine which psychological trait (will, feelings or thoughts) dominates each character, and they must determine the nature of this trait.

A difficulty can arise in doing this if there is more than one character with the same trait, for example, several evil characters, as in *King Lear*. However, by defining precisely which psychological trait is dominant and the precise nature of this trait, one can find the different expressions of this evil. One character might be dominated by his thoughts whereas another might be dominated by her feelings. If two evil characters are dominated by feelings, the precise nature of these feelings might differ between characters. These differences must be found and expressed so that each character is unique and yet remains within the scope of the composition of the performance.

One of the more interesting assumptions of Chekhov's system is that the actors can and should play the full range of dramatic characters, from tragic hero to buffoon. To play only one type, for example, to play only tragedy, is very limiting. The power of contrasts is operative here in that one's ability to play comedy is greatly enriched if one can also play tragedy. To illustrate this point, Chekhov deals with four specific types of performances: Tragedy, Drama, Comedy and Clowning.

When one undergoes a tragic experience in everyday life, one feels psychologically and physically exposed to certain forces or powers that are stronger than one's self. This tragic experience takes possession of the person and produces a sensation that is as if, *"Something* powerful is now present side by side with me, and *It* is independent of me to the same degree that I am dependent upon *It*."[24] A person, or a character in a play, may suffer intensely, but Chekhov says that this intensity of suffering alone is only drama, not yet tragedy. The presence of this powerful "Something" is necessary before intense suffering becomes tragic.

With these statements as a base, Chekhov builds a technique for the actor to use in playing a tragic role. Explaining this technique, he says:

> All an actor has to do when preparing a tragic part is imagine, all the time he is on the stage (while rehearsing or later acting before an audience), that "Something" or "Somebody" is *following* him, driving his character to fulfill its tragic business and to speak his tragic lines. The actor must imagine, or rather sense, this "Something" or "Somebody" as being much, much more powerful than his character and even himself. It should be a kind of *superhuman Presence!* The actor must allow this "Double-ganger" (literally, double-walker)—this specter, wraith or apparition—to act *through* the character which inspires it.[25]

The benefits of this technique are many. It allows the actor to express the tragic essence of the character without exaggerating. It allows the actor to avoid the tendency to inflate himself artifically in order to achieve the grandeur of tragedy. Using this imaginary presence allows the performer to have a sense of truth without becoming naturalistic.

The traits or qualities of this superhuman presence are left open to the actor's creative imagination and the needs of the play and character. Some plays supply this presence for the actor. Chekhov cites the Furies in *The Eumenides*, the witches in *Macbeth*, Mephistopheles in *Faust* and the ghost of Hamlet's father as examples. But if this presence is not indicated by the play, it is up to the actor to play freely with this presence in order to take full advantage of it.

Playing drama requires a very different technique. With drama the actor remains within the bounds of his own human ego. There is no need for the presence of another being. With drama the actor needs only to be well prepared and remain true within the given circumstances of the play.

Playing comedy is similar to drama except that a comic character usually has a predominant psychological feature. This psychological feature needs to be clearly expressed, but performed with inner truth. The actor should never attempt to be funny in order to get big laughs. Chekhov says that "humor that is true, humor of good taste, can be achieved only with complete effortlessness, by means of the greatest possible ease and strong radiations."[26]

Chekhov adds that it is important for the actor playing comedy to radiate in all directions and fill the theatre with rays of happiness and gaiety. These radiations should start before the actor's entrance so that the effort to radiate is not made after the actor is on stage. If the entire cast is radiating this way, a very strong comic atmosphere will be established to which the audience will respond positively.

A quick tempo is another condition of comedy that should be added to the feeling of ease and radiation. However, one has to be careful not to sustain a quick tempo throughout the performance. An unvarying quick tempo is counterproductive and loses the audience's attention. To make the quick tempo effective, the actor must vary it from time to time by suddenly slowing it up or interjecting a short, expressive pause. These variations will act as pleasant shocks to the audience and allow it to enjoy the prevailing quick tempo of the performance.

Clowning is the opposite extreme of tragedy. A truly great clown is also possessed by a "Doubleganger" while performing, but it is a different type than the one found in tragedy. As the tragedian is pursued by a superhuman being, the clown is possessed by a subhuman being, which takes possession of his body and psychology. There may be one or many of these subhuman beings that take possession of the clown, but these beings must be amusing and appealing. They can never have traits that would make the clown repulsive to the audience. Chekhov says that the actor can find rich material for creating such beings in genuine folk and fairytale literature.

There is an important difference between a comedian and a clown. The actor in a comedy reacts naturally to the circumstances and stimulation in the play and his psychological transitions are always justifiable. However, the clown's reactions to the circumstances are unjustified, unnatural and often unexpected. Transitions for the clown require no psychological justification and are spontaneous, quick, often happening without any visible reason. In spite of this, the clown must believe in what he feels and does, and maintain a sense of truth based on the workings of the subhuman being who possesses him.

As extreme as clowning is, it can be an invaluable resource for the actor who performs different types of plays. Clowning develops self-confidence and the actor's sense of truth. Perhaps most importantly, "Clowning will awaken within you that eternal *Child* which bespeaks the trust and utter simplicity of all great artists."[27]

Chekhov offers several systematic ways to approach a role that are based on his system of acting. The first is to approach the part through use of the imagination. To do this the actor must first read the entire script several times to get familiar with the play as a whole. Then the actor concentrates on his part only, imagining each scene until he can see the inner life and outer appearance of the character. One can do this either by seeing the character based on the author's description or by seeing one's self as the character in makeup and costume.

Next the actor cooperates with this image of the character by asking it questions about moments in the play. This is the process mentioned earlier in our discussion of the imagination. After rehearsals begin, the actor should incorporate all that is learned from the director and other actors at rehearsal into the imagination work done between rehearsals. For example, the actor can take a suggestion made by the director in a particular scene and then perform this scene in the imagination, attempting to incorporate the suggestion. This private work will facilitate the actor's work in rehearsal and help free him from inhibitions. Images are free of inhibitions because they are the direct products of the actor's creative individuality. The actor's artistic intuition will tell him when this imagination work has served its purpose. It should not be relied on too heavily. If it does not meet all the actor's needs in developing the character, another approach should be used in conjunction with it.

Another possible approach is to begin preparation work by focusing on atmospheres. To do this the actor imagines the character performing actions and speaking lines within the different atmospheres in the play. Then the actor should choose one of these atmospheres and begin to act in it. While performing in a given atmosphere, one needs to be sure that everything is in harmony with it. This process should be repeated with every atmosphere in the play. It is helpful if the actor can fall in love with the atmospheres of the play, as Stanislavsky stressed at the Moscow Art Theatre. This love of atmospheres enables the actor to see and feel things that remain obscure to others and allows him to develop many important features and fine nuances in the character which would not be there otherwise.

Beginning with the sensation of feelings is another approach available to the actor. The actor first defines the general and most characteristic quality or qualities for the character. Once these qualities are defined and the actor has experienced the sensation of the desirable feelings, he should try to act the part under the influence of this sensation. If the actor finds that the sensations used to awaken the creative feelings are not correct, they should be altered until the actor is entirely satisfied. The actor should then divide the role into sections, the fewer the better, and then rehearse one section at a time. Chekhov reiterates that the qualities and sensations are means of awakening the actor's artistic feelings. When these feelings are awakened, the actor should give himself up to them entirely, a means which will lead to the fulfillment of the role.

The next approach Chekhov suggests is to approach the part using psychological gesture. At first the actor should try to find a psychological gesture for the entire part. If this cannot be done, then minor psychological gestures should be explored until the overall one becomes clear. The actor should start acting on the basis of the psychological gesture and, if it does not seem to work, adjust it until it fits the actor's interpretation of the role. The actor should consider the strength, type, quality and tempo of the gesture while developing it. The psychological gesture should be used in the actor's private work throughout rehearsals and be exercised before each entrance. The actor should define the general tempos of the play and practice the psychological gesture according to these tempos. The contrast between inner and outer tempos should be explored as much as possible. When used as an approach to a part, the psychological gesture also helps the actor discover how the character reacts differently to different characters on the stage. The result is that "the application of the PG [psychological gesture] affords the unique opportunity of painting your part in various colors, thus making your performance rich in tone and fascinating to watch."[28]

An actor may also approach the character using the imaginary body and imaginary center, either together or separately. The actor writes down all business and movement of the character, no matter how insignificant. Then the actor works through these movements using what he discovers about the character while exploring the imaginary body and center. The next step is to add lines to the movement, only a few at first, but eventually rehearsing the entire role. Keep in mind that the imaginary body and center also affect the actor's psychology. In addition, they will reveal nuances of speech that will be appropriate for the character. Chekhov says that through this approach, "the whole width and breadth of the character will unveil before you as a panorama in the *shortest time*. But do not drop your 'game' until the character has been so absorbed by you that you no longer need to think of your imaginary body and center."[29] Chekhov also suggests that some of the laws of composition mentioned earlier might be used as an approach to a character.

Chekhov's final suggestion for approaching a part is to integrate Stanislavsky's units and objectives with his own system as described in *To the Actor*. Although Chekhov's acting system is quite different from the one Stanislavsky developed, much of it is based on Stanislavsky's, and in spite of their differences, Chekhov continually pays homage to what he learned from Stanislavsky. Chekhov's belief in Stanislavsky's approach is evidenced by his comments concerning the use of units and objectives as an approach to a role.

> Units and Objectives are perhaps his [Stanislavsky's] most brilliant inventions, and when properly understood and correctly used they can lead the actor immediately to the very core of the play and the part, revealing to him their construction and giving him a firm ground upon which to perform his character with confidence.[30]

In applying Stanislavsky's units and objectives to Chekhov's system, one should divide the entire play into units using Chekhov's principles discussed in "Composition of the Performance." Thus, the actor first divides the play into three large units and then finds smaller units within these large ones.

Applying objectives to Chekhov's system is more complex. Chekhov first takes exception to Stanislavsky's contention that the superobjective of the play is often not found until the actor is performing before an audience. As a result, the actor must work only from minor objectives not always knowing exactly where they will lead. Chekhov contends that the actor must know the superobjective from the beginning in order to merge all minor objectives into a logical and coherent system.

There are various ways of finding superobjectives of the part and the entire play. First, most characters wage a fight throughout the play; they are in conflict with someone or something. By the end of the play, the character has either won or lost his battle. One way of discovering the superobjective of the character is to ask: "What becomes of the character, what does he do or intend to do *after* he has achieved his victory? What *would* he do if he won his fight, what *should* he do?"[31] Answers to questions such as these will help lead the actor to the character's superobjective. For example, if one were to ask what Willie Loman *(Death of a Salesman)* would do if he were successful in his fight with his destiny, a possible answer would be that Willie would become the most banal type of salesman, like Dave Singleman, whom Willie idolizes in the play. If this is the case, a superobjective for Willie Loman might be: "I want to live like that old Dave Singleman."[32] The actor should be free enough in this exploration of the superobjective to consider his first impression only as a possibility and to explore many superobjectives until he finds one that suits him.

Now that the actor has a grasp on the superobjective of the character, he can pursue smaller objectives with greater success than if the superobjectives were not known. But first he must identify the superobjective of the entire play as well as the character itself. To do this the actor follows the same procedure described above, but instead of asking questions of the character, the actor asks questions of an imaginary audience.

The actor and director ask the imaginary audience several questions about the play, but the most important one deals with the psychological result the audience experiences after the play is over. The actor and director use their imaginations to penetrate the hearts of the audience members to see what these spectators take home with them after the performance. Answers to questions posed to this imaginary audience will provide a basis for defining the play's superobjective.

The same results cannot be achieved by asking the author about the superobjective because a performance is always an interpretation of the play by the actor and director. As a result, the audience's reaction to the play will reveal more about the superobjective than the author's intentions. The psychology of the audience differs vastly from that of the actor and director. The reason for this is:

> Because the audience as a *whole* senses the play with its *heart* and not with its brain; because it cannot be lead astray by the actor's, director's or author's personal points of view, because its reaction on opening night is immediate, free of any tendencies and unconditioned by outside influences; because the audience does not analyze but *experiences;* because it never remains indifferent to the *ethical* value of the play (even when the author himself intends to remain impartial); because it never loses itself in details or evasions, but intuitively detects and savors the very marrow of the play.[33]

Chekhov says that Vakhtangov's productions were always filled with details that communicated clearly to the audience because he never directed without imagining an "ideal" audience attending his rehearsals. Vakhtangov always anticipated this "ideal" audience's reactions and followed its suggestions.

Chekhov stresses that this use of the imagined audience's reaction is not meant to diminish the importance of the actor's and director's interpretation of the play, or for these artists to become overly subservient to the audience. It is a process of cooperation with the audience that guides the actor's and director's interpretation: "The audience is an active co-creator of the performance. It *has* to be consulted before it is too late, and especially when searching for the superobjective of the play."[34]

This is another example of the tremendous importance of the audience in Chekhov's system of acting. With Chekhov's system, an actor never simply plays to the audience. As one can see from these statements, the audience is part of the process of creating the role, and in performance becomes the actor's collaborator.

Once this work with the imaginary audience produces a superobjective for the entire play, the actor may proceed with the identification of the smaller objectives. But Chekhov cautions the actor not to use the reasoning mind in deciding upon these objectives. If an objective is defined through reasoning, it will remain cold and difficult to use. An objective must spring from the entire psychology, so that the emotions, will, and even the body are filled with the objective.

If we strongly desire something in everyday life, we become possessed by the desire, by an inner activity, until we get what we want or realize that we will not be able to get it. The same thing should happen on the stage when using objectives. The actor should be possessed by the objective, so that it permeates his body and psychology. That is why we cannot rely only on reasoning to define the objective, because if we do, we will be thinking the objective and not wanting it. During performance the actor must not wait passively for the moment in the play when the objective is fulfilled, which will happen if the actor's body and psychology are not possessed by the objective.

If the actor feels the objective is not working properly, he may repeat the objective over and over in his mind. This usually does not work, according to Chekhov, because it is a mental process that does not arouse the will. A better alternative is to use a psychological gesture to get over the difficulty with the objective.

Chekhov suggests that another useful way to overcome difficulty with objectives is to imagine the character being possessed by the objective. If the actor peers attentively into the inner life of the character, he will find himself being possessed by the objective.

Chekhov suggests that the actor use those methods of approaching a part that work best and provide the quickest results. Some will be more suitable to a particular character than others. The actor should not overload himself with more than is necessary for the best performance of the character. Reiterating his position that acting should be enjoyable and permeated with a feeling of ease, Chekhov says, "The method must, above all, *help* you and make your work pleasant, and if properly used will not under any circumstances make it hard and depressing. For acting should ever be a joyous art and never enforced labor."[35]

In concluding *To the Actor* Chekhov makes a strong case for the necessity of studying the art of acting. It is unfortunate that such a case needs to be made, but the acting profession is filled with those who feel that they have natural talent and that any study of acting techniques is unnecessary. However, Chekhov makes his case well. All of his reasons do not need to be repeated here. It is enough to say that Chekhov advocates convincingly the need for an objective technique to develop and support an actor's talent.

Chekhov also talks about the reasons for accepting his own system of acting. The first thing he says is to be gained from his system is a professional way of thinking and responding to one's own creative work and the work of others. This system gives the actor a complete terminology, a way of talking about what works and does not work on the stage. With this terminology, one does not need to rely on vague and inadequate terms such as natural, conversational, arty, good, bad, etc. The concrete terminology of Chekhov's system replaces these inadequate terms and it also sharpens the actor's ability to perceive theatrical impressions. In other words, it helps the actor to know what is wrong or right and why. As a result, the actor will become more objective and constructively critical about his own work and the work of others.

Another reason Chekhov gives for the validity of his system is that his technique will facilitate and hasten the actor's work. If his technique is practiced diligently and patiently, Chekhov says it will provide a firm basis for acting and allow the actor to work quickly when he needs to.

In addition, if the system is practiced so that one grasps its principles, it will make the actor's creative intuition work more freely and create an ever-widening scope for its activities. Chekhov says that he built his system on the physical and psychological conditions required by the creative intuition itself. In this regard, he says, "The chief aim of my explorations was to find those conditions which would best and invariably call forth that elusive will-o'-the-wisp known as inspiration."[36]

Chekhov's final reason for the system's acceptance is that it provides the actor with a balance between the practical and impractical. Chekhov says that our materialistic age has caused people to focus almost entirely on what is practical and ignore the intangible powers and qualities of life. An undue emphasis on the commonplace causes all kinds of problems in society; for example, people suffer breakdowns, or seek cheap thrills through fads or drugs. But it is the arts that suffer most from this imbalance. An actor can never successfully cling to what is practical and tangible and at the same time ignore what is impractical and intangible. Chekhov's system provides the means for the actor to keep his feet on the ground and yet rise above it. Ensemble, Feeling, Atmospheres, Radiation, and Laws of Composition are all intangibles, yet they exist on stage as concretely as the actor himself. The exercises Chekhov provides are practical ways to develop technique. They are practical exercises often geared to produce intangibles. In summation, Chekhov says:

> There is not a single exercise in this method which does not serve two purposes at once: to put the actor even more firmly on a *practical* ground and at the same time give him a sound balance between tangible and intangible, between exhaling and inhaling, and thus rescue him from banalities and from artistic suffocation. [37]

In considering Chekhov's acting system as a whole, his final point for the validity of his acting system cannot be stressed enough. As I stated earlier the realities of the materialism and commercialism of the West were difficult for Chekhov to handle. He constantly fought against these destructive forces. His quixotic spirit drove him to find a theatre and audience that wanted to create art and see it created on stage. He felt that it was the interpretation of life that was the actor's mission, and he refused to accept the possibility that the materialistic world view of the West could kill that mission.

Mikhail Chekhov's system of acting manages to preserve the artistic aspect of the actor's work. It is filled with references and allusions to the creative forces that exist within human beings. It is an optimistic system that asks the actor to reach for the highest realm of creativity and expression. At the same time, it provides the actor with a practical and even logical means to reach these heights. But its practicality is only a means to the impractical. Its logic only makes it clear that intangibles exist and allows us to understand how to reach them.

In dealing with Chekhov's system of acting, one must always remember his early statements that the actor's psychology consists of feelings and desires as well as thought. The rational mind is not ignored, but it must always function along with the emotions and desires of the artist. The use of logical reasoning in Chekhov's system is always inferior to the use of the imagination. Our imaginations and creative individualities are the rich resources that allow the body and psychology to express a character on stage.

Mikhail Chekhov seems to be getting more attention now than at any other time since his death in 1955. The studios in New York that teach his system are proving to be successful, and a recent issue of *The Drama Review* is totally devoted to Chekhov. [38] As people continue to realize the importance of his contributions and the benefits of using his techniques, Chekhov's influence is bound to spread.

Part of the process of understanding Chekhov's techniques is gaining an understanding of the man behind those techniques. Chekhov's acting system is in many ways an extension of himself. His vivid imagination led him to emphasize the development and use of the actor's creative imagination over a dependence on the actor's personal life and observations. The hardships

Chekhov experienced in his personal life, brought about by political and sociological forces beyond his control, led him to advocate a theatre that dealt with political and sociological issues. His interest in religion and philosophy led him to probe the depths of inspiration and higher forms of consciousness. His love for humanity was strong, in spite of the ways in which he was abused by others during the early periods of his life.

Other actors and directors have striven for many of the same artistic goals Chekhov mentions. However, Chekhov gives us unique ways of achieving these goals. His concepts of radiation, psychological gesture and the uses of the imagination are perhaps the most interesting of his acting techniques. But the most unique and inspiring aspect of Chekhov's system is his emphasis on human love. This love and the belief that there is some good in every individual in spite of how unsympathetic they may seem on the surface, led him to emphasize human love in many ways throughout his acting system. It permeates every aspect of the actor's technique.

The commercialism of the acting profession in this country creates many obstacles to creativity and art. It also creates such an emphasis on success that often our humanity is lost in the morass of fighting for parts and making a living in an overcrowded profession. Chekhov provides a way to keep one's humanity in one's art, regardless of the occurrences in everyday life. He provides a way for us all to be more expressive of ourselves, be more creative, and truly interpret life in all its complexities and richness.

Notes

Chapter 1

1. Mikhail Chekhov, "Zhizn' i vstrechi," *Novyi zhurnal* 7 (1944), 5.

2. Chekhov, *Novyi zhurnal* 7 (1944), 21.

3. Chekhov, *Novyi zhurnal* 7 (1944) 5–19. The entire account of Mikhail Chekhov's experiences with his father that follows is taken from this section of *Novyi zhurnal*.

4. Michael Chekhov, "Death Portrayed Falsely on Stage, Says Chekhov," *New York World Telegram*, 2 March 1935.

5. Chekhov, *Novyi zhurnal* 7 (1944), 18–19.

6. Personal interview with Ford Rainey, 16 January 1982.

7. Chekhov, "Death on Stage."

8. Personal interview with Mala Powers, 14 January 1982.

9. Interview with Mala Powers.

10. Chekhov, *Novyi zhurnal* 8 (1944), p. 20.

11. Johannes Hemleben, *Rudolf Steiner: A Documentary Biography* (Sussex: Henry Goulden Ltd., 1975), p. 108.

12. Hemleben, *Rudolf Steiner*, p. 109.

13. Chekhov, *Novyi zhurnal* 8 (1944), 20–22.

14. Chekhov, *Novyi zhurnal* 8 (1944), p. 24.

15. Chekhov, *Novyi zhurnal* 8 (1944), 25.

16. Interview with Mala Powers. The following discussion of Anthroposophy comes from this interview.

17. Interview with Mala Powers.

18. Hemleben, *Rudolf Steiner*, p. 110.

19. Hemleben, *Rudolf Steiner*, p. 111.

20. Michael Chekhov, *To the Actor on the Technique of Acting* (New York: Harper & Row, 1953), pp. 96–102.

21. Chekhov, *To the Actor,* p. 100.

22. Chekhov, *Novyi zhurnal* 132 (1978), 151.

23. Leonard Stanton, "Optina Pustyn': A Sketch of Its History and Spiritual Tradition," Diss. University of Kansas 1983, p. 12.

24. Stanton, pp. 15–16; see also John Meyendorff, *St. Gregory Palamas and Orthodox Spirituality* (New York: St. Vladimir's Seminary Press, 1974), p. 38.

25. Chekhov, *Novyi zhurnal* 8 (1944), 38–45.

Chapter 2

1. Mikhail Chekhov, "Zhizni' i vstrechi," *Novyi zhurnal* 7 (1944), 23–24.

2. Nancy Anne Kindelan, "The Theatre of Inspiration: An Analysis of the Acting Theories of Michael Chekhov," Diss. University of Wisconsin-Madison 1977, p. 1.

3. Chekhov, *Novyi zhurnal* 7 (1944), 29–33.

4. Douglas Gilbert, "Noted Actor Haunted by the Reputation of His Famous Uncle," *World-Telgram,* n.d., Chekhov Clipping File, Library and Museum of Performing Arts, Lincoln Center, New York, New York.

5. Michael Chekhov, *To the Director and Playwright,* Charles Leonard, ed. (Westport, Conn.: Greenwood Press, 1977), p. 51.

6. Chekhov, *To the Director and Playwright,* p. 39.

7. M. Knebel', "Arkhiv Mikhaila Aleksandrovicha Chekhova," *Teatr,* No. 6 (1981), 97–98.

8. Marc Slonim, *Russian Theatre from the Empire to the Soviets* (New York: Collier Books, 1962), p. 297.

9. Knebel', *Teatr,* p. 98.

10. Slonim, *Russian Theatre,* pp. 196–97.

11. Slonim, *Russian Theatre,* p. 198.

12. Slonim, *Russian Theatre,* pp. 198–99.

13. Slonim, *Russian Theatre,* p. 108.

14. Constantin Stanislavsky, *My Life in Art* (New York: Theatre Arts Books, 1948), pp. 534–35.

15. P. Markov, "Pervaja studija MXT," in *Pravda teatra* (Moscow: Iskusstva, 1965), p. 256.

16. Markov, *Pravda teatra,* p. 270.

17. Markov, *Pravda teatra,* pp. 275–78.

18. Slonim, *Russian Theatre,* pp. 286–87. Beginning in 1913, Vakhtangov also worked with an independent student group called Mansurov Studio. In 1917, this group was known as Vakhtangov's Studio and in 1920 it became known as the Third Studio of the Moscow Art Theatre. Four years after Vakhtangov's death, this theatre was renamed the Vakhtangov Theatre and it remains one of Moscow's leading companies.

19. William L. Kuhlke, "Vakhtangov's Legacy," Diss. State University of Iowa 1965, see chapter VII, Fantastic Realism.

20. Kuhlke, "Vakhtangov's Legacy," p. 111. This quotation comes from notes taken by Zakhava and Kotlubai in a meeting with Vakhtangov in April of 1922, the year of Vakhtangov's death. These notes are included in Vendrovskaia's editions of Vakhtangov's notes and letters.

21. Nikolai A. Gorchakov, *The Theatre in Soviet Russia* (New York: Columbia University Press, 1958), pp. 246–47.

22. Gorchakov, *Theatre in Soviet Russia*, p. 246.

23. For descriptions of this production, see Kuhlke, "Vakhtangov's Legacy," pp. 1–4 and pp. 92–109; Gorchakov, *Theatre in Soviet Russia*, pp. 253–55; Slonim, *Russian Theatre*, pp. 292–94.

24. Kuhlke, "Vakhtangov's Legacy," p. 2.

25. Slonim, *Russian Theatre*, p. 296.

26. Markov, *Pravda teatra*, p. 299.

27. Markov, *Pravda teatra*, pp. 303–7.

28. Gorchakov, *Theatre in Soviet Russia*, p. 247.

29. Markov, *Pravda teatra*, p. 308.

30. Gorchakov, *Theatre in Soviet Russia*, p. 250.

31. Markov, *Pravda teatra*, pp. 310–12.

32. Markov, *Pravda teatra*, p. 312.

33. Markov, *Pravda teatra*, p. 312.

34. Gorchakov, *Theatre in Soviet Russia*, p. 250.

35. Slonim, *Russian Theatre*, p. 298.

36. Gorchakov, *Theatre in Soviet Russia*, pp. 256–63.

37. Gorchakov, *Theatre in Soviet Russia*, p. 261.

38. Personal interview with Mala Powers, 14 January 1982.

39. Gorchakov, *Theatre in Soviet Russia*, pp. 259–60.

40. Slonim, *Russian Theatre*, pp. 295–99.

41. Mel Gordon, Introd., *Lessons to the Professional Actor*, by Michael Chekhov, ed. Deirdre Hurst du Prey (New York: Performing Arts Journal Publications), p. 15.

42. Chekhov, *Novyi zhurnal* 9 (1944), 21–26.

43. Chekhov, *Novyi zhurnal* 9 (1944), 22.

44. Chekhov, *Novyi zhurnal* 9 (1944), 29.

45. Chekhov, *Novyi zhurnal* 9 (1944) 28–29; see also Kindelan, *Theatre of Inspiration*, pp. 108–10.

46. Chekhov, *Novyi zhurnal* 9 (1944), 29–30.

47. Chekhov, *Novyi zhurnal* 9 (1944), 30.

Chapter 3

1. Mikhail Chekhov, "Zhizn' i vstrechi," *Novyi zhurnal* 10 (1945), 28.

2. Oscar G. Brockett and Robert R. Findlay, *Century of Innovation* (Englewood Cliffs, NJ: Prentice-Hall, Inc., 1973), p. 334.

3. Chekhov, *Novyi zhurnal* 10 (1945), 22–23.

4. Brockett and Findlay, *Century of Innovation*, p. 334.

5. Personal interview with Deirdre Hurst du Prey, 21 January 1982.

6. Michael Chekhov, *Chekhov Theatre Studio—Dartington Hall* (England: Curwen Press, 1936), pp. 30–31.

7. Program from the Moscow Art Players production at the Majestic Theatre. From the personal files of Mala Powers.

8. Announcement for the Moscow Art Players production. From the personal files of Mala Powers.

9. Program from the Moscow Art Players production at the Shubert Theatre. From the personal files of Mala Powers.

10. Shubert Theatre program.

11. Personal interview with Beatrice Straight, 15 January 1982.

12. Interview with Deirdre Hurst du Prey.

13. Chekhov, *Dartington Hall,* pp. 8–9.

14. Chekhov, *Dartington Hall,* p. 10.

15. Harold Clurman, *The Fervent Years* (New York, 1957), pp. 157–58.

16. Clurman, *The Fervent Years,* p. 158.

17. Chekhov, *Dartington Hall,* p. 11.

18. Interview with Deirdre Hurst du Prey.

19. Interview with Deirdre Hurst du Prey.

20. Chekhov, *Dartington Hall,* pp. 11–19. The following discussion of the aims of the Dartington Hall Studio is based on material from these pages.

21. Chekhov, *Dartington Hall,* pp. 12–13.

22. Chekhov, *Dartington Hall,* p. 14.

23. Chekhov, *Dartington Hall,* p. 17.

24. Chekhov, *Dartington Hall,* pp. 20–21.

25. Rudolf Steiner, *A Lecture on Eurythmy* (London: Rudolf Steiner Press, 1967), pp. 12–22; see also Rudolf Steiner, *Speech and Drama* (London: Anthroposophical Publishing Co., 1959).

26. Steiner, *Eurythmy,* pp. 16–17.

27. Interview with Beatrice Straight.

28. Personal interview with Paul Rogers, 20 January 1982.

29. See Steiner, *Eurythmy.*

30. Emile Jaques-Dalcroze, *Rhythm, Music and Education,* trans. Harold F. Rubinstein (London: Chatto & Windus, 1921), pp. vii–viii; see also Emile Jaques-Dalcroze, *Eurhythmics, Art and Education,* trans. Frederick Rothwell, ed. Cynthia Cox (New York: A.S. Barnes & Co., 1930).

31. Brockett and Findlay, *Century of Innovation,* p. 203.

32. Interview with Paul Rogers.

33. Interview with Paul Rogers.

34. Chekhov, *Dartington Hall,* p. 22.

35. Chekhov, *Dartington Hall,* p. 24.

36. For a further explanation of Goethe's theory, see Johann Wolfgang von Goethe, *Goethe's Color Theory,* trans. & ed. Herb Aach (New York: Van Nostrand Reinhold Company, 1971).

37. Chekhov, *Dartington Hall,* p. 27.

38. Interview with Deirdre Hurst du Prey.

39. Interview with Deirdre Hurst du Prey.

40. Interview with Deirdre Hurst du Prey.

41. Michael Chekhov, *Chekhov Theatre Studio* (Ridgefield, Conn.: The Chekhov Theatre Studio Inc., 1939), p. 14.

42. Chekhov *Theatre Studio,* p. 5.

43. Nancy Anne Kindelan, "The Theatre of Inspiration: An Analysis of the Acting Theories of Michael Chekhov," Diss. University of Wisconsin-Madison 1977, p. 189.

44. Chekhov, *Theatre Studio,* pp. 6–7.

45. Oliver M. Sayler and Marjorie Barkentin, "Chekhov Theatre Productions, Inc., Chartered to Give Plays on Broadway," Press release part of the Michael Chekhov Clipping File, Lincoln Center Library for the Performing Arts, New York, New York.

46. Oliver M. Sayler and Marjorie Barkentin, "Chekhov Theatre Takes Lyceum for Dostoievsky's 'The Possessed' Opening Tuesday Ocrober 24," Press release part of the Michael Chekhov Clipping File, Lincoln Center Library for the Performing Arts, New York, New York.

47. Kindelan, *Theatre of Inspiration,* p. 189.

48. Brooks Atkinson, "The Possessed," *New York Times,* 25 Oct. 1939, p. 36, col. 2.

49. Atkinson, "The Possessed."

50. Kindelan, *Theatre of Inspiration,* p. 191.

51. Personal interview with Ford Rainey, 16 January 1982.

52. Interview with Deirdre Hurst du Prey.

53. Brooks Atkinson, "Twelfth Night," *New York Times,* 3 Dec. 1941, p. 32, col. 2.

54. See reviews of "Chekhov Evening" produced by Chekhov Theatre Productions. Michael Chekhov Clipping File, Lincoln Center Library for the Performing Arts, New York, New York.

55. Interview with Deirdre Hurst du Prey.

56. See: Michael Tschechow, *Werkgeheimnisse der Schauspielkunst,* (Zurich: Werner Classen Verlag, 1979). This is Georgette Boner's German translation of Chekhov's *To the Actor,.* She has added a chapter on Chekhov's work and an explanation of her involvement with the book.

57. Interview with Deirdre Hurst du Prey.

58. Interview with Deirdre Hurst du Prey.

59. In 1946 Chekhov was still condemned by the Soviet government. However, his popularity among the public was very strong. As a result, copies of the book were cherished in the Soviet Union, but to this date the book is still not well known there. I showed a copy to Victor Rozov, the contemporary Soviet playwright, when he visited the University of Kansas in the fall of 1978. He had never seen the book and was thrilled with its contents. He said the only word to describe Mikhail Chekhov was "genius."

60. Interview with Ford Rainey.

61. Herbert Cohn, "Michael Chekhov Bids for Oscar with Warm 'Spellbound' Portrait," *Daily Eagle,* 16 Dec. 1945, n. pag. Michael Chekhov Clipping File, Lincoln Center Library for the Performing Arts, New York, New York.

62. Interview with Mala Powers and John Dehner. See also Kindelan, p. 7.

63. Interview with Mala Powers.

64. Mala Powers, "Michael Chekhov, an Intimate Glimpse," pp. 2–3. From the personal collection of Mala Powers.

65. Powers, "Intimate Glimpse," p. 6.

66. Personal interview with John Dehner, 17 January 1982.

67. Interview with John Dehner.

68. Fred Lawrence Guiles, *Norma Jean, The Life of Marilyn Monroe* (New York: McGraw-Hill, 1969), pp. 116–17. For other references to Marilyn Monroe's relationship with Chekhov, see: Maurice Zolotow, *Marilyn Monroe* (New York: Harcourt, Brace & Co., 1960).

69. Marilyn Monroe, *My Story* (New York: Stein and Day, 1974), p. 133.

70. Guiles, *Norma Jean,* p. 118.

71. Monroe, *My Story,* pp. 133–34.

72. Monroe, *My Story,* pp. 134–35.

73. Monroe, *My Story,* p.135.

74. Guiles, *Norma Jean,* p. 316.

Chapter 4

1. Personal interviews with Deirdre Hurst du Prey, 21 January 1982 and with John Dehner, 17 January 1982.

2. Personal interview with Paul Rogers, 20 January 1982.

3. Michael Chekhov, *To the Actor on the Technique of Acting* (New York: Harper and Row, 1953), pp. 2-6.

4. Chekhov, *To the Actor,* p. 2.

5. Chekhov, *To the Actor,* p. 5.

6. Michael Chekhov, "Love in Our Profession," introd. John Dehner, recorded 1955, Hollywood, California, Lincoln Center Library for the Performing Arts, New York, New York. See also, Michael Chekhov, *To the Director and Playwright,* comp. Charles Leonard (Westport, Conn.: Greenwood Press, 1963), chapter 3, "Love in Our Theatre: Art or Profession." My sources for all notes referring to lectures are the tapes themselves. In *To the Director and Playwright,* Charles Leonard has included edited transcriptions of some of the recorded lectures. I refer the reader to these edited transcriptions where appropriate.

7. Chekhov, "Love in Our Profession."

8. Michael Chekhov, "Ensemble Feeling," introd. John Dehner, recorded 1955, Hollywood, California, Lincoln Center Library for the Performing Arts, New York, New York. See also Chekhov, *To the Director and Playwright,* chapter 11, "Toward Better Ensembles."

9. Chekhov, "Ensemble Feeling."

10. Chekhov, *To the Actor,* p. 5.

11. Chekhov, *To the Actor,* pp. 5-6.

12. Chekhov, *To the Actor,* p. 6.

13. Chekhov, *To the Actor,* p. 11.

14. Personal interview with Eddie Grove, 20 January 1982.

15. Chekhov, *To the Actor,* p. 10.

16. Personal interview with Ford Rainey, 16 January 1982.

17. I observed Mr. Grove's acting class in New York City, 22 January 1982.

18. Chekhov *To the Actor,* p. 12.

19. Personal interview with Beatrice Straight, 15 January 1982.

20. Chekhov, *To the Actor,* p. 10.

21. Chekhov, *To the Actor,* p. 15.

22. Michael Chekhov, "Great Russian Directors, Part I," introd. John Dehner, recorded 1955, Hollywood, California, Lincoln Center Library for the Performing Arts, New York, New York. See also Chekhov, *To the Director and Playwright,* p. 47.

23. Chekhov, *To the Actor,* p. 17.

24. Richard Schechner, as quoted in Jennifer Dunning, "The New American Actor," *The New York Times Magazine,* 2 October 1983, p. 36.

25. "The New American Actor," pp. 35-37, 68-74.

Chapter 5

1. Michael Chekhov, "Characterization, Part II," introd. John Dehner, recorded 1955, Hollywood, California, Lincoln Center Library for the Performing Arts, New York, New York.

2. Michael Chekhov, *To the Actor on the Technique of Acting* (New York: Harper & Row, 1953), p. 23.

3. Chekhov, *To the Actor,* p. 23.

4. Chekhov, *To the Actor,* p. 25.

5. Chekhov, "Characterization," Part II."

6. Chekhov, *To the Actor,* p. 28.

7. Chekhov, *To the Actor,* p. 36.

8. Vasili O. Toporkov, "Physical Actions," *Actors on Acting,* ed. Toby Cole and Helen Krich Chinoy (New York: Crown Publishers, Inc., 1970), p. 527.

9. Chekhov *To the Actor,* pp. 40–41.

10. Chekhov, "Ensemble Feeling." See also, Chekhov, *To the Director and Playwright,* chapter 11, "Toward Better Ensembles."

11. Chekhov, *To the Actor,* p. 41.

12. Chekhov, "Ensemble Feeling."

13. Michael Chekhov, "Many-Leveled Acting," introd. John Dehner, recorded 1955, Hollywood, California, Lincoln Center Library for the Performing Arts, New York, New York. See also Chekhov, *To the Director and Playwright,* chapter 15, "Many-Leveled Performances."

14. Chekhov, *To the Actor,* p. 48.

15. Chekhov, *To the Actor,* p. 50.

16. Chekhov, *To the Actor,* p. 51.

17. Chekhov, *To the Actor,* pp. 51–53.

18. Chekhov, "Many-Leveled Acting."

19. Chekhov, *To the Actor,* p. 53.

20. Chekhov, "Love in Our Profession."

21. Chekhov, *To the Actor,* p. 98.

22. Chekhov, "Many-Leveled Acting."

23. Chekhov, *To the Actor,* p. 99.

24. Chekhov, *To the Actor,* p. 100.

25. Susanne K. Langer, *Feeling and Form* (New York: Charles Scribner's Sons, 1953), pp. 143–45.

26. Langer, *Feeling and Form,* p. 146.

27. Chekhov, *To the Actor,* pp. 58–59.

28.   Chekhov, *To the Actor,* p. 59.

29.   Chekhov, *To the Actor,* p. 65.

30.   Chekhov, *To the Actor,* pp. 64, 65.

31.   Chekhov, *To the Actor,* p. 71.

32.   Chekhov, *To the Actor,* p. 73.

33.   Chekhov, *To the Actor,* p. 75.

34.   Chekhov, *To the Actor,* pp. 76–79.

35.   Robert Pasolli, *A Book on the Open Theatre* (New York: Avon Books, 1970), pp. 4–8. See also Cole and Chinoy, *Actors on Acting,* pp. 663–69.

36.   Pasolli, *Open Theatre,* p. 3.

37.   Chekhov, *To the Actor,* p. 83.

38.   Michael Chekhov, "Monotony," introd. John Dehner, recorded 1955, Hollywood, California, Lincoln Center Library for the Performing Arts, New York, New York.

Chapter 6

1.   Chekhov, "Characterization," Part I, introd. John Dehner, recorded 1955, Hollywood, California, Lincoln Center Library for the Performing Arts, New York, New York. See also Chekhov, *To the Director and Playwright,* chapter 8, "Character Structure and Motivation."

2.   Chekhov, "Characterization," Part I. See also, Chekhov *To the Actor,* p. 86.

3.   Chekhov, *To the Actor,* p. 87.

4.   Chekhov, "Characterization," Part I.

5.   Chekhov, "Characterization," Part I.

6.   Chekhov, *To the Actor,* p. 89.

7.   Chekhov, *To the Actor,* p. 91. Here Chekhov makes a clear distinction between the character as a whole and characterization. In his lectures, no such distinction is made, and characterization is used to refer to the process of transforming the actor.

8.   Chekhov, *To the Actor,* p. 92.

9.   Chekhov, "Characterization," Part II.

10.   Chekhov, "Characterization," Part II.

11.   Chekhov, *To the Actor,* pp. 96–97.

12.   See chapter 1, "Anthroposophy," pp. 7–11.

13.   Personal interview with John Dehner.

14.   Chekhov, *To the Actor,* p. 101.

15.   Chekhov, *To the Actor,* p. 101.

16.   Chekhov, "Many-Leveled Acting." See also Chekhov, *To the Director and Playwright,* p. 107.

17. Chekhov, *To the Actor,* p. 103.

18. Chekhov, *To the Actor,* p. 105.

19. Chekhov, *To the Actor,,* p. 111.

20. Chekhov, *To the Actor,* p. 112.

21. For further discussions of Chekhov's rehearsal techniques, see Michael Chekhov, "On Rehearsal" and "Short-cuts to Acting," introd. John Dehner, recorded 1955, Hollywood, California, Lincoln Center Library for the Performing Arts, New York, New York. See also Chekhov, *To the Director and Playwright,* chapter 12, "Toward Better Rehearsals."

22. Chekhov, *To the Actor,* p. 12.

23. Chekhov, *To the Actor,* p. 124.

24. Chekhov, *To the Actor,* p. 138.

25. Chekhov, *To the Actor,* pp. 138–39.

26. Chekhov, *To the Actor,* p. 140.

27. Chekhov, *To the Actor,* p. 144.

28. Chekhov, *To the Actor,* p. 152.

29. Chekhov, *To the Actor,* pp. 153–54.

30. Chekhov, *To the Actor,* p. 154.

31. Chekhov, *To the Actor,* p. 158.

32. Chekhov, *To the Actor,* pp. 158–59.

33. Chekhov, *To the Actor,* p. 161.

34. Chekhov, *To the Actor,* p. 162.

35. Chekhov, *To the Actor,* p. 170.

36. Chekhov, *To the Actor,* p. 176.

37. Chekhov, *To the Actor,* p. 178.

38. See, "Michael Chekhov," *The Drama Review* 27, No. 3 (Fall 1983).

Bibliography

Books

Billington, James H. *The Icon and the Axe.* New York: Random House, 1970.

Bradshaw, Martha, ed. *Soviet Theatres, 1917–1941.* New York: Research Program on the U.S.S.R., 1954.

Brockett, Oscar, and Robert R. Findlay. *Century of Innovation: A History of European and American Theatre and Drama Since 1870.* Englewood Cliffs, N.J.: Prentice-Hall, 1973.

Carter, Huntly. *The New Theatre and Cinema of Soviet Russia.* New York: International Press, 1925.

————. *The Spirit of the Russian Theatre, 1917–28.* London: Brentano's Ltd., 1929.

————. *The Theatre of Max Reinhardt.* London, 1914.

Chekhov, Michael. *Chekhov Theatre Studio.* Ridgefield, Conn.: The Chekhov Theatre Studio Inc., 1939.

————. *Chekhov Theatre Studio—Dartington Hall.* England: Curwen University Press, 1936.

————. *Lessons for the Professional Actor.* Deirdre Hurst du Prey, ed. New York: Performing Arts Journal Publications, 1985.

————. *Put' aktera.* Leningrad: Asadeia, 1928.

————. *O tekhnike aktera.* U.S.A.: n.p., 1946.

————. *To the Actor on the Technique of Acting.* New York: Harper & Row, 1953.

————. *To the Director and Playwright.* Charles Leonard, ed. New York: Harper and Row, 1963.

Clurman, Harold. *All People are Famous.* New York: Harcourt, Brace, Jovanovich, 1974.

————. *The Fervent Years; the Story of the Group Theatre and the Thirties.* New York: Alfred A. Knopf, 1945.

Cole, Toby, comp. *Acting: A Handbook of the Stanislavsky Method.* Revised ed. New York: Crown Publishers, Bonanza Books, 1955.

————, ed. *Actors on Acting.* New York: Crown Publishers, 1949.

————, and Helen Kirch Chinoy. *Directors on Directing.* Revised ed. New York and Indianapolis: Bobbs-Merrill Co., Inc., 1963.

Edwards, Christine. *The Stanislavsky Heritage; Its Contribution to the Russian and American Theatre.* New York: New York University Press, 1965.

Freedley, George, and John A. Reeves. *A History of the Theatre.* New York: Crown Publishers, 1966.

Goethe, Johann Wolfgang von. *Goethe's Color Theory.* Trans. and ed. Herb Aach. New York: Van Nostrand Reinhold Company, 1971.

Gorchakov, Nikolai A. *Theatre of Soviet Russia.* Trans. Edgar Lehrman. New York: Columbia University Press, 1957.

Gorchakov, Nickolai M. *Stanislavsky Directs*. Trans. Miriam Goldina. New York, 1954. Rpt., New York: Minerva Press, 1968.

———. *Vakhtangov School of Stage Art*. Trans. G. Ivanov-Mumjiov, Ed. Phyllis Griffin. Moscow Foreign Publishing House, n.d.

Gromov, V. *Mikhail Chekhov*. Moskva: Iskusstva, 1970.

Guiles, Fred Lawrence. *Norma Jean, The Life of Marilyn Monroe*. New York: McGraw-Hill, 1969.

Hemleben, Johannes. *Rudolf Steiner, a Documentary Biography*. Trans. Leo Twyman. Sussex, England: Henry Goulden, Ltd., 1975.

Hingley, Ronald. *The Russian Mind*. New York: Charles Scribner's Sons, 1977.

Houghton, Norris. *Moscow Rehearsals: The Golden Age of Soviet Theatre*. New York, 1926. Rpt., New York: Grove Press, Inc., 1962.

Jaques-Dalcroze, Emile. *Eurhythmics, Art and Education*. Trans. Frederick Rothwell. Ed. Cynthia Cox. New York: A. S. Barnes & Co., 1930.

———. *Rhythm, Music and Education*. Trans. Harold F. Rubinstein. London: Chatto & Windus, 1921.

Kindelan, Nancy A. "The Theatre of Inspiration: An Analysis of the Acting Theories of Michael Chekhov." Diss. University of Wisconsin-Madison, 1977.

Kovalevsky, Pierre. *St. Sergius and Russian Spirituality*. Trans. W. Elias Jones. Crestwood, N.Y.: St. Vladimir's Seminary Press, 1976.

Kuhlke, William L. "Vakhtangov's Legacy." Diss. State University of Iowa, 1965.

Langer, Susanne K. *Feeling and Form*. New York: Charles Scribner's Sons, 1953.

Lawrence, John. *A History of Russia*. 6th ed. 1957. Rpt., New York: Meridian Books, 1978.

Magarshack, David. *Stanislavsky: A Life*. New York: Chanticleer Press, 1951.

Markov, P.A. "Pervaja studija MXT." In *Pravda Teatra*, pp. 249–322. Moscow: Iskusstva, 1965.

———. *The Soviet Theatre*. London: Victor Golancz, Ltd., 1934.

Meyendorff, John. *Byzantine Hesychasm: Historical, Theological and Social Problems*. London: Variorum Reprints, 1974.

———. *Byzantine Theology*. New York: Fordham University Press, 1979.

———. *The Orthodox Church*. Trans. John Chapin. New York: Pantheon Books, 1962.

———. *St. Gregory Palamas and Orthodox Spirituality*. Trans. Adde Fiske. Crestwood, N.Y.: St. Vladimir's Seminary Press, 1975.

Meyerhold on Theatre. Trans., Ed., and commentary by Edward Braun. New York: Hill and Wang, 1969.

Monroe, Marilyn. *My Story*. New York: Stein & Day, 1974.

Moore, Sonia. *The Stanislavsky System: The Professional Training of the Actor*. New York, 1965; Rpt. New York: Viking Press, 1966.

Munk, Erika, ed. *Stanislavsky and America*. Greenwich, Conn.: Fawcett Publishing, Inc., 1967.

Nemirovich-Danchenko, Vladimir. *My Life in the Russian Theatre*. Trans. John Cournos. Boston: Little, Brown, and Co., 1936.

Pasolli, Robert. *A Book on the Open Theatre*. New York: Avon Books, 1970.

Saylor, Oliver. *Inside the Moscow Art Theatre*. New York: Brentano's, 1955.

———. *The Russian Theatre*. New York: Little, Brown and Co., 1920.

———. *Russian Theatre under the Revolution*. Boston: Little, Brown and Co., 1920.

Slonim, Marc. *Russian Theatre: From the Empire to the Soviets*. New York: Crowell-Collier Publishing Co., Collier Books, 1962.

Stanislavsky, Constantin. *An Actor Prepares*. Trans. Elizabeth Reynolds Hapgood. New York: Theatre Arts, Inc., 1936.

———. *Building a Character*. Trans. Elizabeth Reynolds Hapgood. New York: Theatre Arts, Inc., 1949.

————. *Creating a Role.* Trans. Elizabeth Reynolds Hapgood. New York: Theatre Arts, Inc., 1961.

————. *My Life in Art.* Trans. J. J. Robbins. 5th ed. London: Geoffrey Bles, 1948.

————. *The Sea Gull Produced by Stanislavsky.* Trans. David Magarshack. Ed. S. D. Balukhaty. New York: Theatre Arts Books, 1952.

————. *Stanislavsky Produces Othello.* Trans. Dr. Helen Norwalk. London: Geoffrey Bles, 1948.

Stanton, Leonard. "Optina Pustyn': A Sketch of Its History and Spiritual Tradition." Diss. University of Kansas, 1983.

Steiner, Rudolf. *Anthroposophical Leading Thoughts.* Trans. George and Mary Adams. London: Rudolf Steiner Press, 1926.

————. *The Evolution of the Consciousness as Revealed through Intuition and Knowledge.* 2nd ed. Trans. V. E. W. and C. D. Letchworth, Hertfordshire, 1926; rpt. London: Rudolf Steiner Press, 1960.

————. *A Lecture on Eurythmy.* London: Rudolf Steiner Press, 1967.

————. *Rudolf Steiner, an Autobiography.* Trans. Vita Stebbing. Ed. Paul M. Allen. Blauvelt, N.Y.: Rudolf Steiner Publications, 1977.

————. *Speech and Drama.* Trans. Mary Adams. London: Anthroposophical Publishing Co., 1959.

————. *Theosophy; An Introduction to the Supersensible Knowledge of the World and Destination of Man.* 18th ed.; New York: AnthropoSophic Press, 1923.

Tairov, Alexander. *Notes of a Director.* Trans. and Introd. William Kuhlke. Coral Gables, Fl.: University of Miami Press, 1969.

Tschechow, Michael. *Werkgeheimnisse der Schauspielkunst.* Trans. Georgette Boner. Zurich: Werner Classen Verlag, 1979.

Tschizewskij, Dmitrij. *Russian Intellectual History.* Trans. John C. Osborne. Ed. Martin P. Rice. Ann Arbor, Mich.: Ardis, 1978.

Varneke, Bernard V. *History of the Russian Theatre, Seventeenth through the Nineteenth Century.* Trans. Boris Brasol. Ed. Belle Martin. New York: The Macmillan Co., 1951.

Zolotow, Maurice. *Marilyn Monroe.* New York: Harcourt, Brace and Co., 1960.

Periodicals

Belyi, Andre. "The Man, Rudolf Steiner as Stage-Director and Actor." *Journal for Anthroposophy,* 27 (Spring 1978), 27–37.

Chekhov, Mikhail. "Pis'ma M. A. Chekhova." *Novyi zhurnal,* 132 (1978).

————. "Zhizn' i vstrechi." *Novyi zhurnal,* vols. 7–11 (1944–45).

Knebel', M. "Arkhiv Mikhaila Aleksandrovicha Chekhova." *Teatr,* No. 6 (1981), 97–100.

"Michael Chekhov." *The Drama Review,* 27 (Fall 1983).

Woloschin, Margarita. "Michael Chekhov: The Actor as Conscious Artist." *Journal for Anthroposophy,* 27 (Spring 1978).

Newspapers

General

Bakshy, Alexander. "Apropos of the Russian Season." *New York Times,* 24 February 1935.

Chekhov, Michael. "Death Portrayed Falsely on Stage, Says Chekhov." *New York World Telegram,* 2 March 1935.

Dunning, Jennifer. "The New American Actor." *The New York Times Magazine,* 2 October 1983.

Gilbert, Douglas. "Noted Actor Haunted by the Reputation of His Famous Uncle." *New York World Telegram,* n.d.

"Michael Chekhov Restored as U.S.S.R. Theatre Luminary." *Variety,* 9 July 1969, p. 27, col. 3.

Morrow, Honoré. "Adventure in Devon." *The Christian Register,* 15 April 1937.

"Moscow Sends a Sample of Its Theatre." *New York Herald Tribune,* 10 February 1935.

"Portrait." *The New York Times,* 2 July 1946.

Reviews

"Abbie's Irish Rose." *The New York Times,* 23 December 1946, p. 19, col. 4.

Atkinson, Brooks. "Chekhov Doubleheader—Michael Chekhov Makes Debut in English in 'Anton Chekhov Sketches.'" *The New York Times,* 28 September 1942.

_____. "The Possessed." *The New York Times,* 25 October 1939, p. 26, col. 2.

_____. "Twelfth Night." *The New York Times,* 3 December 1941, p. 32, col. 2.

Brown, John M. "Michael Chekhov Brilliant in Two Chekhov Sketches." *New York World Telegram,* 28 September 1942.

Cohn, Herbert. "Michael Chekhov Bids for Oscar With Warm 'Spellbound' Portrait." *Brooklyn Daily Eagle,* 16 December 1945.

"Cross My Heart." *The New York Times,* 19 December 1946, p. 42, col. 3.

Freedly, George. "Chekhov Amuses Russian Audiences." *New York Morning Telegraph,* 28 September 1942.

"Holiday for Sinners." *The New York Times,* 20 September 1952, p. 13, col. 2.

"In Our Time." *The New York Times,* 12 February 1944, p. 11, col. 2.

"Invitation." *The New York Times,* 30 January 1952, p. 22, col. 6.

Pollock, Arthur. "Michael Chekhov Plays in English." *Brooklyn Daily Eagle,* 29 September 1942.

"Rhapsody." *The New York Times,* 12 March 1954, p. 17, col. 1.

"Song of Russia." *The New York Times,* 11 February 1944, p. 17, col. 2.

"Specter of the Rose." *The New York Times,* 2 September 1946, p. 12, col. 4.

"Spellbound." *The New York Times,* 2 November 1945, p. 22, col. 2.

Waldolf, Wilella. "Michael Chekhov and Company in Anton Chekhov's Sketches." *New York Post,* 28 September 1942.

Tapes

Taped lectures of Mikhail Chekhov speaking to the Hollywood Society of Film Actors are part of the Chekhov collection located at the Lincoln Center Library for the Performing Arts, New York, New York. The following titles, introduced by John Dehner, were recorded in 1955 and broadcast in 1965 by KPFK-FM in Los Angeles.

"Characterization, Parts I & II"
"Ensemble Feeling"
"Shortcuts to Acting"
"Great Russian Directors, Parts I & II"
"Many-Leveled Acting"
"Monotony"
"Love in Our Profession"
"On Rehearsal"

Interviews

Dehner, John. Personal interview. 17 January 1982.
du Prey, Deirdre Hurst. Personal interview. 21 January 1982.
Grove, Eddie. Personal interview. 20 January 1982.
Powers, Mala. Personal interview. 14 January 1982.
Rainey, Ford. Personal interview. 16 January 1982.
Rogers, Paul. Personal interview. 20 January 1982.
Straight, Beatrice. Personal interview. 15 January 1982.
Zhdanov, Georgy Semenovich. Personal interview. 15 January 1982.

Index